Excavating the Unconscious © ZPJ Fox 2024
Reproduction in any manner, in whole or in part,
in English or any other language, or otherwise,
without the written permission of the copyright holder is prohibited.

Art by Ziji *landscapeoftheheart.com*

For information address
zijiartmethod@pm.me
@zijiartpoems

The moral right of the author has been asserted. All rights reserved. Without limiting the rights under copyright restricted above, no part of this publication may be reproduced, stored in, or introduced into a retrieval system, or transmitted, in any form or by any means (electronic, mechanical, photocopying, recording or otherwise), without the prior written permission of both the copyright owner and the publisher of this book.

Two Spirit Endnote #1 p177

ABOUT THE AUTHOR

Ziji is a writer, visual artist and for a time a Playback Theatre actor and director. He has four kids, seven grandchildren and is in the 30th year of his second marriage. He lives in the rainforest of the Northern Rivers.

He has worked as a clinical psychologist for over fifty years specialising in trauma and relationships. Now retired, he has a part time practice in couple therapy.2

He has developed this arts and poetry practice that though not intended, has had a therapeutic effect unearthing discarded body memories, some his own and others of generational trauma and healing.[1] This book is part memoir for my family and close friends.

---

[1] 'It is also true that memory sometimes comes to him as a voice. It is a voice that speaks inside him, and it is not necessarily his own. It speaks to him in the way a voice might tell stories to a child, and yet at times this voice makes fun of him, or calls him to attention, or curses him in no uncertain terms. At times it wilfully distorts the story it is telling him, changing the facts to suit its whims, catering to the interests of drama rather than truth. Then he must speak to it in his own voice and tell it to stop, thus returning it to the

Front cover [2] poem

So much beauty here
the quiet vulnerability almost hurts
to feel your body ache with love's
longing for rest, reaches into my heart
where the mystery of you unfolds.
Is it me or you unbounded,
melted into one, on my knees?
Ziji 15/03/23

---

silence it came from. At other times it sings to him. At still other times it whispers. And then there are the times it merely hums, or babbles, or cries out in pain. And even when it says nothing, he knows it is still there, and in the silence of this voice that says nothing, he waits for it to speak.' Paul Auster in The Invention of Solitude 1982

[2] Poor image reproduction throughout is all my doing. They look better in a digital version. On the back cover, the painting on the easel behind me is by my friend Nome, who also took the photo – hence the smile!

NOW

Observed and written by Cassie Douglas of heartcraftcreative.com

Outside a gentle, dappled light creeps over the ferns and the autumn breeze makes the palms dance. Music fills the space, which is warm and comfortable and there at the centre, is Saskia, still and naked. Aside from the scratching of Ziji's pencils on paper, the space is quiet, insular, womb-like.

The atmosphere requires very few or no words. The silence carries its own kind of energetic communication between artist, muse, and the work.

Essentially this is a 1:1 life drawing session, yet the process is very different. Most life drawing sessions do not allow for a relationship between artist and model. Therefore, the experience is more objective and to a degree, emotionally distant.

In a regular life-drawing session, the model tends to look away from the face of the artist. However, in this room, an intense and intimate relationship flourishes, allowing a birth of original art that is raw and primitive. Both artist and model bring equally creative elements to the session.

Before pencil meets paper or a single piece of clothing is removed there is a deep checking in process that occurs between artist and muse. Without this checking in process, the practice and the work are at risk of inauthenticity. There is also the chance that both artist and muse may have a misaligned creative experience.

And so, the checking in process begins. Ziji and Saskia face one another. They allow themselves to come to a grinding halt and breathe. In these few minutes, there is only one goal: to be as grounded and present as possible. It is not a verbal process, but a sensory one. They scan each other's face, eyes, and breath. He reads her, she reads him. There is an internal sense of what is to come next.

If there is constriction in the nervous system, it is lovingly but directly noted. Because, for the work to come through in the most uncorrupted way, the lines of energy need to be clear. "It is the invisible connections between us that feed the process", Ziji tells me. "I have a connection with Saskia beyond this time when we meet physically. I can feel her, and she feels me".

Saskia Endnote #3

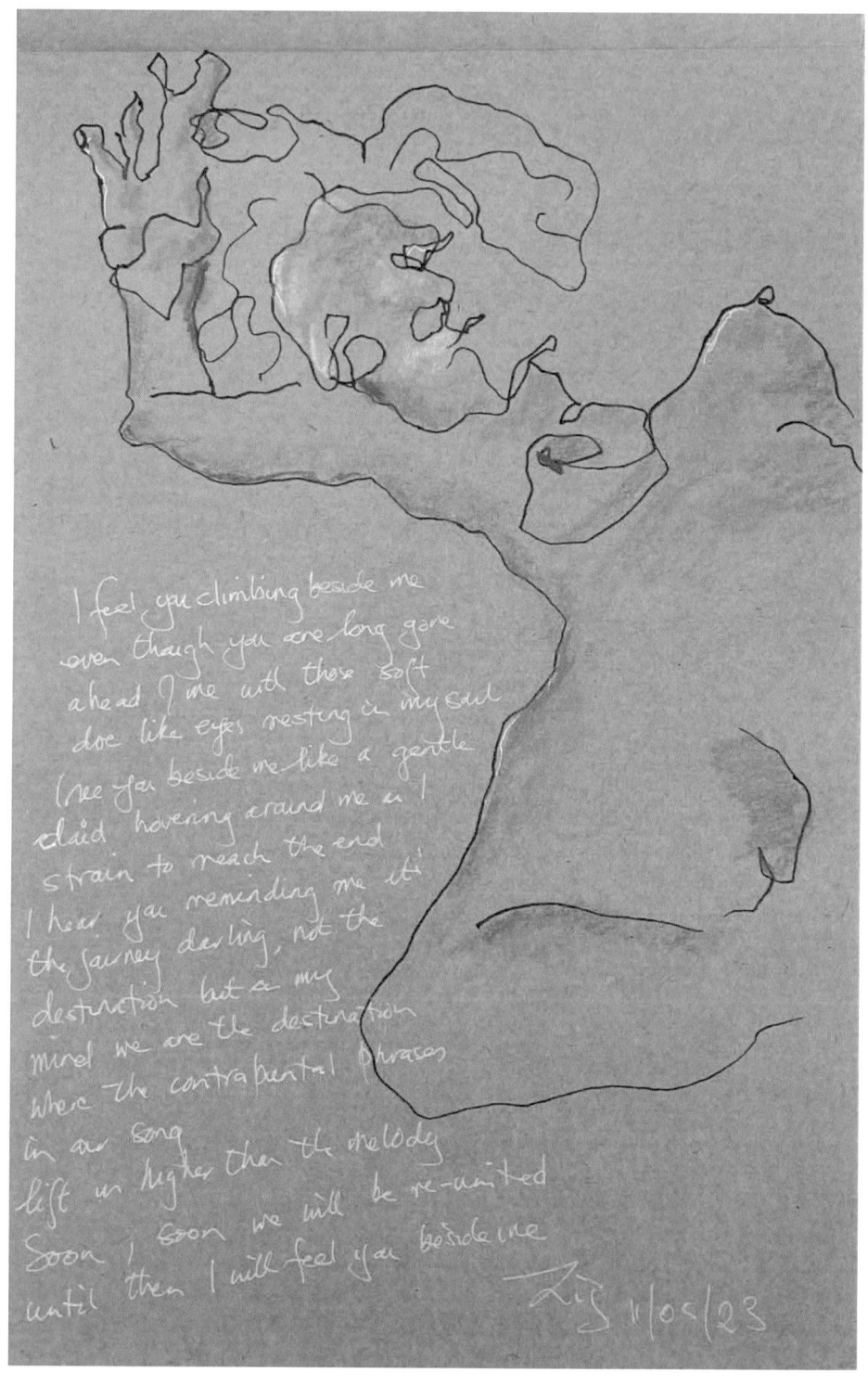

Love song to Mary Endnote #4

*I feel you climbing beside me
even though you are long gone
ahead of me with those soft
doe like eyes resting in my soul
I see you beside me like a gentle
cloud hovering around me as I
strain to reach the end
I hear you reminding me it's
the journey darling, not the
destination but in my
mind we are the destination
where the contrapuntal phrases
in our song
lift us higher than the melody
soon, soon we will be re-united
until then I will feel you beside me
Ziji 11/05/23*

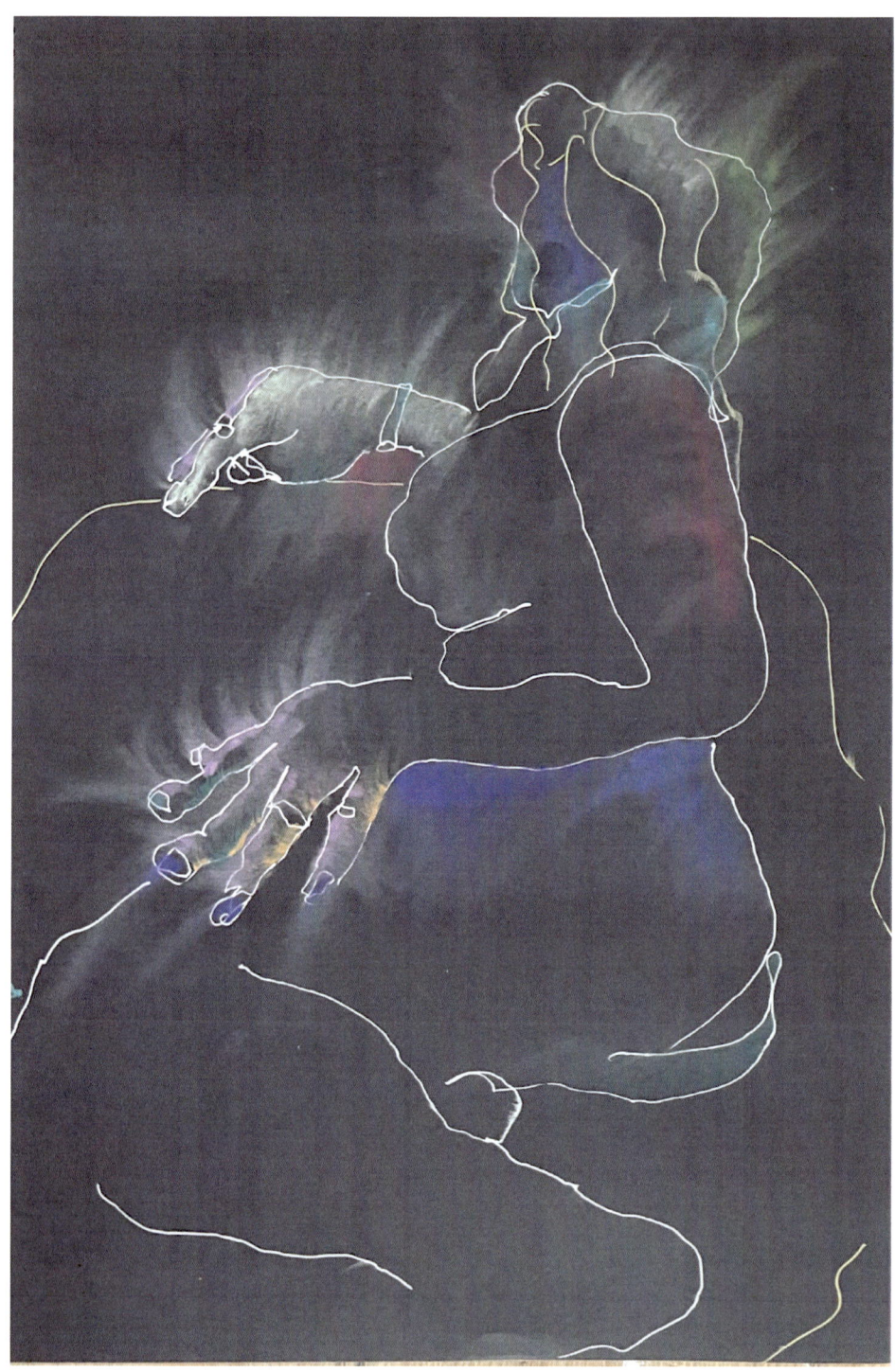

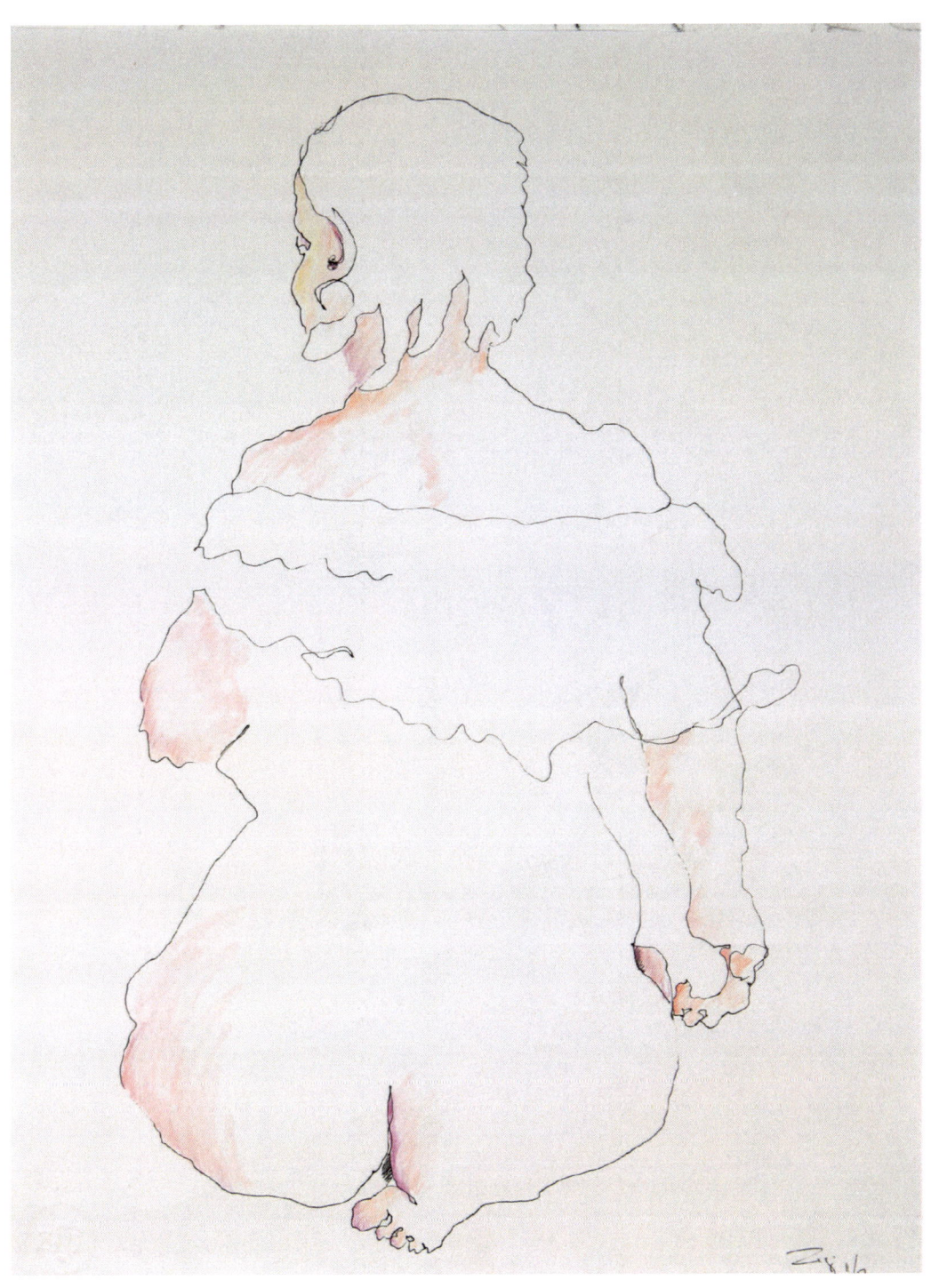

Contour drawing Endnote #5

Group pose at Katherine's 'An Artist Affair'

> *I can see you looking away*
> *you are never invisible to me*
> *just your breath tells me where you are*
> *our energy mingles so freely without boundary*
> *it's as if we are twinned even apart looking away*
> *we will fly back to our nest as surely as any paired doves.*
> *Ziji 21/05/23*

MUSE #6

Saskia is beautiful, confident, and motored by integrity, Ziji has lovingly labelled Saskia the "Queen of Shame" due to her tendency to excavate any large or small energetic constriction in the body. She is professionally and intuitively skilled in the art of seeing through bullshit. She pulls dark things into the light.

For Saskia, it is important that both parties can drop into the body, feel each other and that both can calibrate their nervous systems prior to the creative process. She is committed to, even protective of, Ziji's art practice and his flow. Saskia determines truth by identifying any restriction in the body and naming it before it has a chance to develop.

> *Saskia: "In this space, I know that we share more than I share with clients in my body work practices. We are also intertwined privately. So that gives this a whole other dimension. Nevertheless, when I come here, my intention is to leave my own shit outside, as best as I can. Because the truth is that I tend to feel everything all the time. Sometimes it's difficult to leave something at the door, while still being authentic, but I think I manage it well. I will speak on some of what is going on for me, but not necessarily on all of it, because this place is not the space for that".*

> *Ziji: "The thing about Saskia and I is that we're both quite complicated people who appear incredibly simple. But we really get each other's complexity and contradictions and it's completely okay. I have a lot of internal contradictions and so does she".*

> *Saskia: "I feel that we are not any different from anyone else. I think what may possibly differentiate us from other humans that we are willing to look. That's the piece. I believe everyone is multifaceted, but we choose to look. Ziji and I want to know, and we want to see. And that's where the integrity and the curiosity is".*

Occasionally there may be a theme that arises from a dream, or an emotionally significant experience arises within the session that asks for more exploration. Perhaps the underlying theme is to consistently unearth whatever is hiding. Saskia's specialty! Often, she explores what Ziji comes to her with, with great curiosity. She sees if she can find that thing within herself. If it is an emotion he wants to explore, she goes to where that emotion is in her. Essentially, they use each other as a mirror.

Self. Endnote #7

> and now I will make
> my face forever a play
> of multiple candlelights
> gleaming and deceiving
> so no one will see & feel
> what has broken.
> In some light it will even
> appear transformed and
> made whole
> and not even a lover
> will divine the
> broken sex, the
> eviscerated heart
> and the soul's longing
> to move on from
> this.
> Ziji 28/02/23

In other art classes, models may attempt to evoke creativity and variety using a particular pose, but here it is peeled right back, to absolute intuitive movement. There are no predetermined poses and Saskia simply moves with what is natural, feeling into what is good for her body and that is where she goes. Intriguingly, it tends to be exactly what Ziji was looking for. The process is organic and instinctive, and it works.

> *Saskia: "I acknowledge that this way of working was an evolution for the both of us. Initially, I could feel myself approaching an edge of myself, because of the intimacy. As a life model, you are trained to focus on something inanimate. So, when we looked into each other's eyes for an entire pose for the first time, it felt too intimate...because I was used to something different. But we reframed and restructured the intimate space we had set. And after our nervous systems had calibrated in the process, it felt completely normal. Interestingly, it now feels almost off if my gaze is elsewhere. Often, I will check in with Ziji and ask... what are we doing with our eyes? Because we both understand the subtlety of where the eyes are placed. This is a different communication and conversation that is happening and affects what appears on the paper".*
>
> *Ziji: "I suspect artists and their models have been doing and discovering this since the beginning. I don't think we've come up with anything new".[3]*

Ziji holds a palette of pens in one hand, and colours with the other. The fragments of colour are impactful and random in their minimalism.

---

[3] 'The image of woman as a sexualized object in Western culture, expressions of property ownership and wealth in European oil painting, and modern advertising' said Berger in his TV series and in the book of the same name *Ways of Seeing* 1972. https://en.wikipedia.org/wiki/John_Berger It had a profound effect on my growth as a queer white male artist. I am so drenched in western culture's power and my privilege that I doubt I can see without the male gaze. 'The beauty standards perpetuated by the gaze have historically sexualized and fetishized the black female nude due to an attraction to their characteristics but at the same time punished black women and pushed their bodies outside of what is considered desirable' https://en.wikipedia.org/wiki/Male_gaze

In Katherine's art group Endnote #8

Emptiness Endnote #9

*Placing me here with you
is some kind of miracle
dreams and reality
meld one into another
as our souls reach
across the eyes and ears
and meet truly for the
first time
Ziji 01/23*

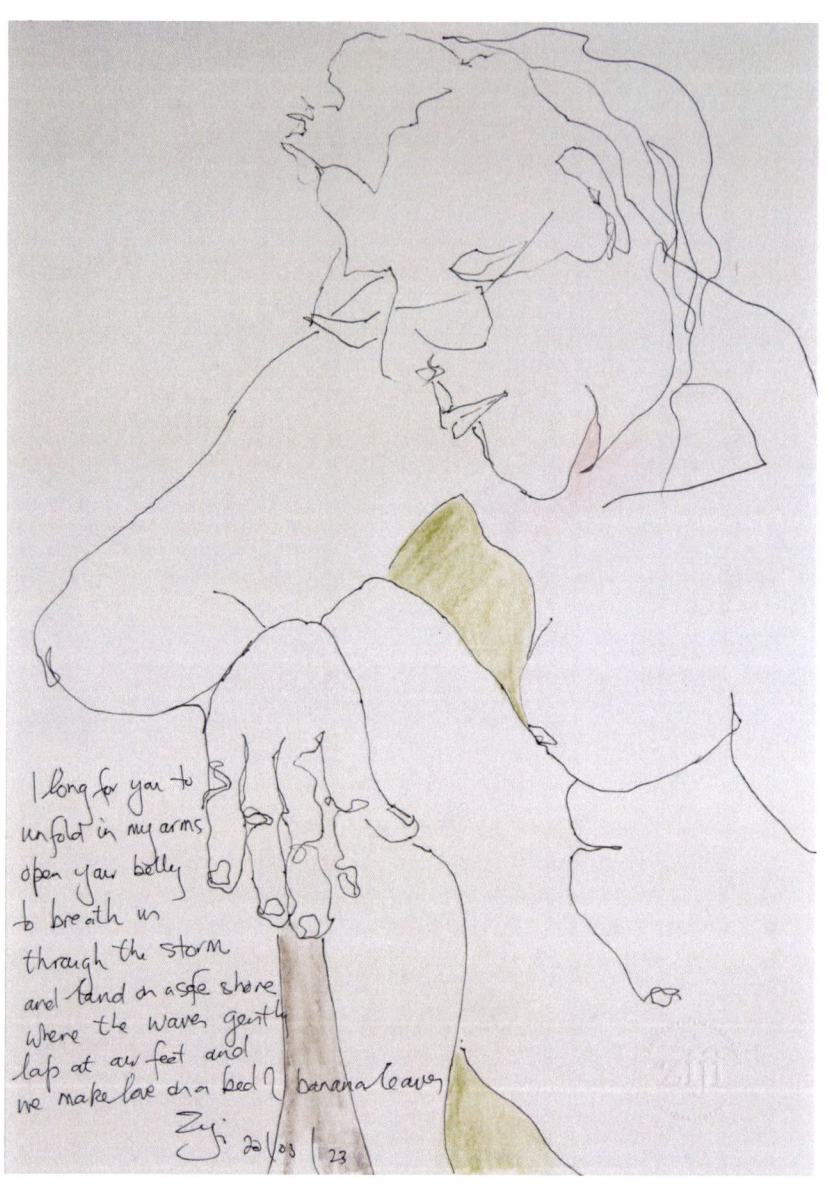

*I long for you to
unfold in my arms
open your belly
to breathe us
through the storm
and land on a safe shore
where the waves gently
lap at our feet and
we make love on a bed of banana leaves
Ziji 20/03/23*

There is no reasoning as to why he chooses the colours he does, and that is the point.

He lets his hand go where it wants to go, and often he catches himself out wanting to intervene with thought or analysis. As soon as that happens, he knows he must step back to not fall into contrived territory.

Too much thinking, too much structure will turn my art into just another piece of shit, he says.

In all the nudity of this process, there is nothing atmospherically sexual. No leaky energy, no trespassing of boundaries. Only a loving commitment by both parties that is driven by healing, creativity, and the removal of layers. It is about seeing. Really seeing.'4

And then deeply buried, confronting images can arise.

Within the place he has created with Saskia, Ziji hopes to step away from the power relationship of the male gaze by exchanging "white, dressed male at desk carefully observing nude female model" with a consensual and participatory process.

Mutually agreed, they both undress for each session, allowing stronger dynamic, heightened sensuality, and most importantly, less objectivity. The concept of objectivity is dragged by its hair from its unconscious shadows into the light.

Ziji may have tapped into a bottomless well of creativity. For him, inspiration and flow never end. This sacred time and practice are

---

[4] I want to critique that view by naming the 'seeing' she observed as a first cousin of the *male gaze* (see footnote 2 above). Inside myself I know the experience of seeing Saskia naked while I am also naked, is pleasurable but not visibly arousing. That lack of excitation might point to scopophilia – 'the sexual pleasure that a person derives from looking …. (at) the nude body... as a substitute for actual participation in a sexual relationship.' https://en.wikipedia.org/wiki/Scopophilia

In 'seeing' I am *other-ing her* and hitching a ride on a scophic process to reach into my own forgetting, that *other* of memory. https://en.wikipedia.org/wiki/Other_(philosophy)

Cinema depiction of love making is a good example of this phenomena. My experience of being the object of a pedophile's gaze is in the mix.

simply allowing the tap to be turned on, full pelt. When the time is up, life resumes, but for now it is a deep exhale from life.

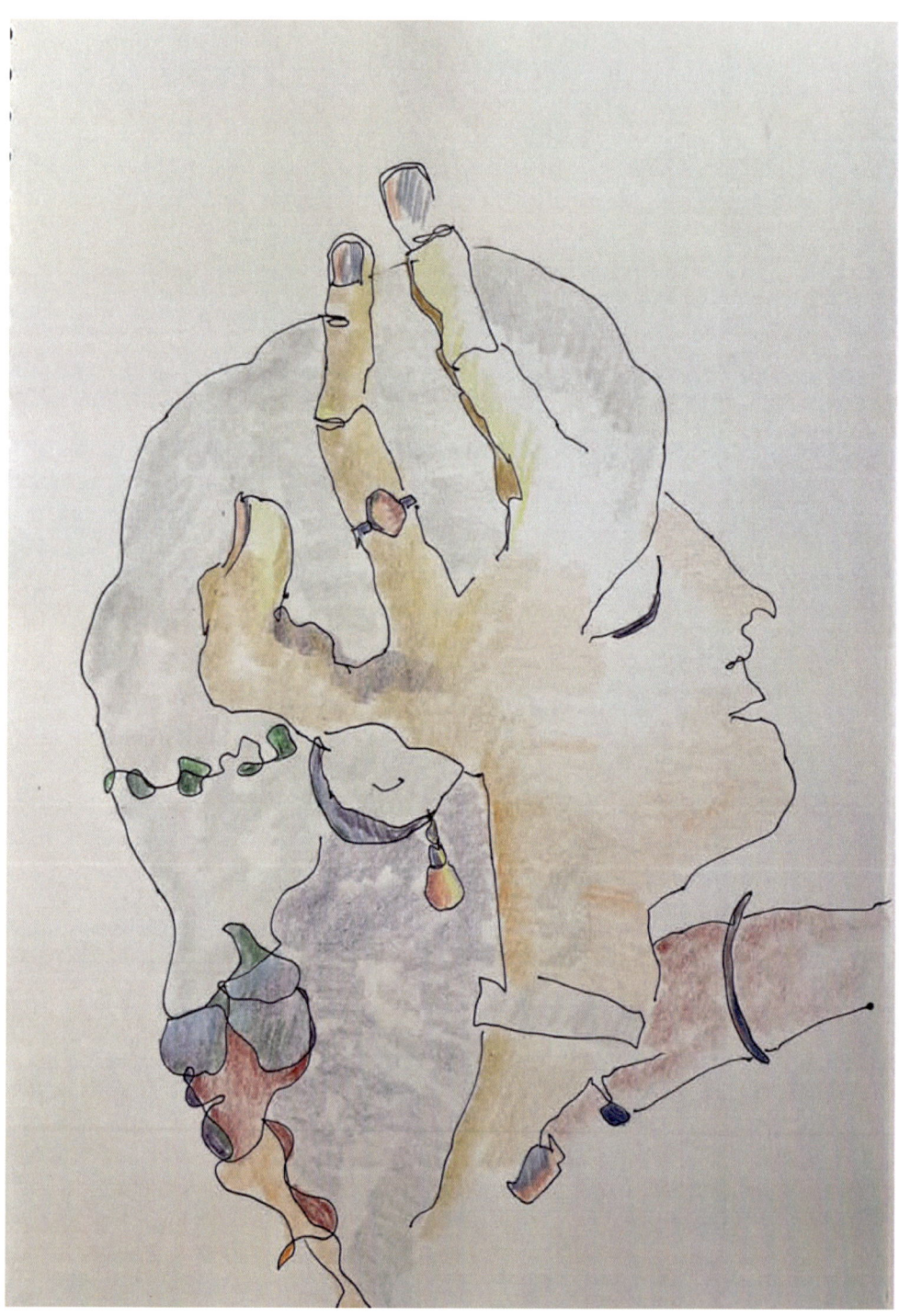

Bridge Endnote #10

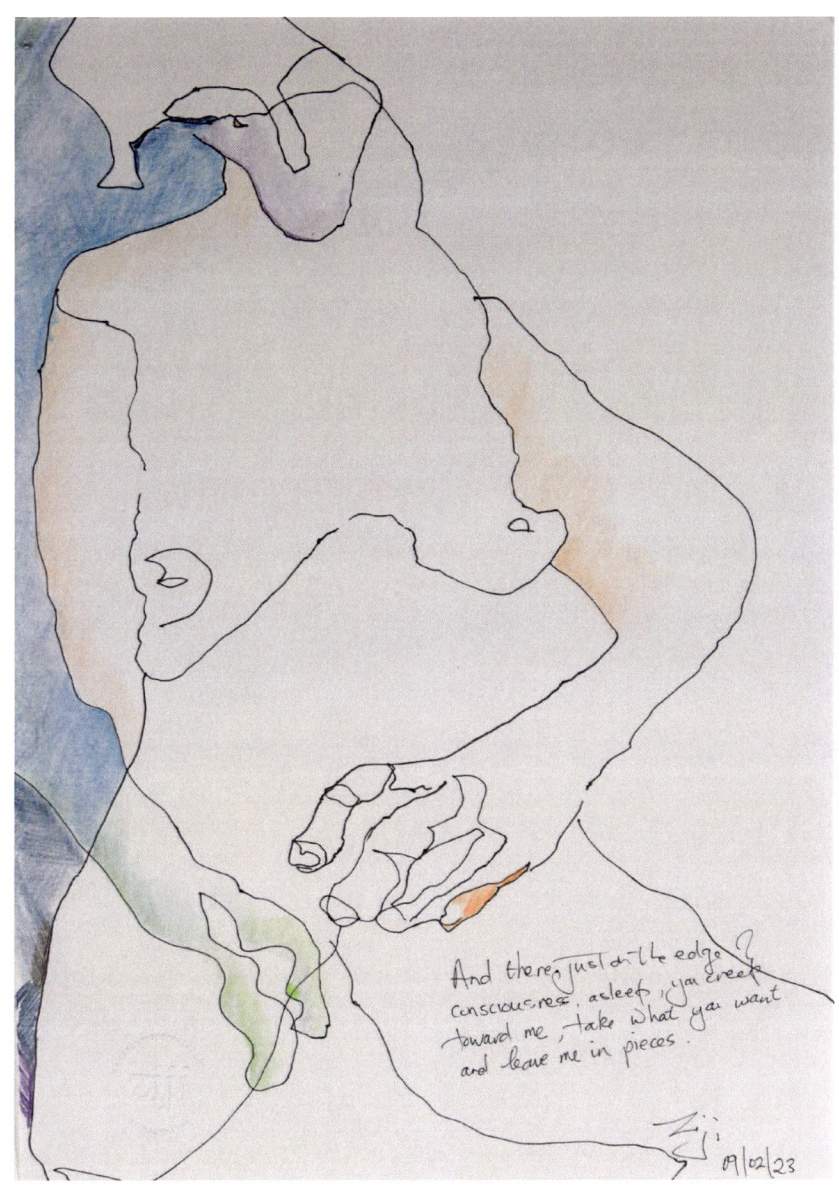

The hand Endnote #11

And there, just on the edge of consciousness, asleep, you creep toward me, take what you want and leave me in pieces.
Ziji 09/02/23

*Life emerging and I
returning always to
where it began. One
breath in and out and I
am restored to who I am
Ziji '21*

Trauma memory Endnote #12

Resting now I am in a daize
not knowing what has been inside
I feel down my chest where his
weight still present like a corpse
dead wait even asleep
I long for that forgetting
forget fullness filled
with emptiness
gone
Ziji 28/02/22

V2P Endnote #13

*This one cry
will be heard around
the world
and the watchers
beyond our time
will wonder what
kind of creatures were
we
swallowing a planet whole
and all who would eat them
finding such profound peace in
beauty and song.
Did these not satisfy them?
Give them hope?
Ziji 18/10/23*

Human Endnote #14

*Such beauty
passes us in the
street and we are
awakened for a moment
to our many blessings
then life intervenes
the atm screams
love comes rushing
like a commodity
and the treasure passes by
I didn't get to say hello
welcome human
we are in this together
Ziji 11/23*

THEN

One way to understand the source of some of my art/poems is the backstory. For example, where does this poem and image on page 21 come from? The title refers to trauma (a much-misused term).

The implied darkness in the poem conflicts with the calm rest of Saskia in the drawing, reminding me that relaxation can be a trauma trigger for children who were abused in their sleep.

What shapes my art/poetry begins before birth, prior to the conception that anticipated my body and the 'flesh of the world' [5], the village I grew in. All stored at a cellular level for later retrieval hopefully before it became my fate. [6] Some of the events reported here are part body memory, transmitted as transgenerational epigenetic inheritance.[7] Some were fed to me through the placenta, the emotions of my mother and of those near to her. [8]

The words she spoke and the songs she sang to me as I grew in her womb. Her hands stroking her expanding abdomen. They continue to exist as a felt sense in my body, and come to life in unexpected ways, including in dreams and in these art/poems. The facts I have retrieved from members of my extended family and my own direct experience.

---

[5] https://en.wikipedia.org/wiki/Maurice_Merleau-Ponty

[6] 'Until you make the unconscious conscious, it will direct your life and you will call it fate.' CG **Jung**

[7] https://www.bbc.com/news/health-25156510

[8] https://www.klinikum.uni-heidelberg.de/fileadmin/zpm/psychiatrie/fuchs/Literatur/The_phenomenology_of_body_memory.pdf

Ear Endnote #15

Un-see Endnote #16

*Taken as one piece we seem
whole.
Underneath we are a multitude
a colony of beings, seeings
like the seasons one shows up
more than another
here a fallen golden leaf
there a sunflower,
fruit swollen and plucked
from aching limbs
and ice in cold beer
snow under children's bare feet.
We are in each place different
and yet the same.
A multitude of crystal facets
celebrating life! l'chaim.
Ziji '21*

In 1944, during the war and five years before I was born, my mother worked at the BBC as a radio announcer. She had left studying medicine in Devon, where she had met my future foster mother Betty, and was living with a Belgian French Catholic named Louis, to whom she fell pregnant. Not revealing her condition, she asked her parents for their blessing to marry.

With their High Church of England morals to defend, Louis was both Catholic and French, and thus beneath what they expected for their daughter. Not having ever known my grandparents, upper class superiority and racism combined, I can't say which was the greater demerit – French or Catholic. Without the blessing of her parents she separated from Louis, gave up her job, returned from London to the family home, and went looking for a husband to avoid being unwed and a single mother, probably without support from her father.

The most likely contender was her first cousin John, whom she had grown up with. They were the children of siblings - as were her own parents. Their two first cousin marriages in a row was a consanguineous union. They were about as related as half siblings. My parents were my first cousins once removed. I am a child of incest.

My father asked her father for permission to marry. Grandfather, a Commander in the Royal Navy, described by their surviving next-door neighbour as a martinet,[9] did not approve. He extracted a promise from my father, a Captain in the British Army Royal Engineers, senior officer to junior officer, gentlemen to gentlemen, to take six months to cool down before asking again. Neither knew of my mother's pregnancy.

Shortly after, and under the pressure of my mum's desperation to not birth a bastard, father agreed to elope, betraying his promise to her father, and thereby manifesting the biblical circumstances where the '*sins of the father are visited upon the sons*'.[10]

---

[9] A rigid military disciplinarian. One who demands absolute adherence to forms and rules.

[10] 'God stores away a man's iniquity for his sons.' Job 21:19

2008 Endnote #17

I try to imagine the conversation between my parents, where she convinced him to elope. I don't think he had much say in it. He was already struggling from a disturbed childhood during WWI. His mother had instituted seances when all her brothers were killed in the madness of regiments being taken from a whole county - thus ensuring that all enlisted men from one family would likely die in the same month or even within a week.

His mother was overcome with grief and obsessed with making contact in the afterlife. Dad was aged between 2 and 6 during this time.

His uncle Lawrence was a psychiatrist. He kept a farm in North Devon where he took some of his patients for rehabilitation. My father was often there in his adolescence. I imagine his uncle noticed Dad's distress, and knew that his sister, Dad's mother had checked out. Together they worked the garden and the fields, and this became a life-long source of calm and recreation for Dad.

As a young adult studying Architecture, one of his student friends told me that Dad witnessed several frightening psychic phenomena. Imagined or real, he was emotionally disturbed by the time he enlisted. He was 27 years old.

He was stationed in the Middle East. Dad told me that the commander of his regiment had beaten him up in the officer's mess as an act of public humiliation. A disciplinary action they would have called it, to make an example of him. The commander had discovered my father was in a sexual relationship with a junior officer. This was a threat to his command. His lover was discharged and sent back to England. My father had a mental breakdown and was hospitalised in the psychiatry ward of an army hospital.

Kenneth 2018 Endnote #18

He was treated there for a couple of months in what sounded like an enlightened program. He then returned to duty in England. He was on home leave the day he and my mum eloped to marry. She miscarried on the wedding night. Dad believed she was a virgin and returned to duty a couple of days later. My mother went home to her mum to recover.

Soon after, they conceived two children: Michael and Madeline. In September 1948 they both died from encephalitis. My brother Michael was three years old, and my sister Madeline was six months old. I have a strange sense of duty to live fully, even abundantly to complete the lives they didn't enjoy. They are perhaps the only two people who can bring tears to my eyes.

My mother, her parents, sister, my dad, and friends buried the kids in Poltimore, Devon, where she would later join them. In the depths of loss and grief, she decided to try again for a baby, threatening Dad that if he would not help, she would go to Southampton and find a merchant marine to assist her.

According to both her sister and my foster mother, Anne, my mum was a charming extrovert, a flirt, and the life of the party. A choral singer, poet and like her mother, a playwright. She was a sickly kid and expelled from two schools allegedly because of inappropriate relationships with other girls.

From the age of 14 her sister covered for her when she had boyfriends. Standing guard outside his bedroom window where my mother had crawled in to spend the evening. This sister was a girl guide, and she became in later years the most influential woman in my life. Naomi.

When Naomi died, she left me the contents of her house in Berkshire U.K. It was a museum in which she had kept everything of her parents and grandparents. There was enough from the proceeds to buy our campervan. We had her registered as 'Naomi'.

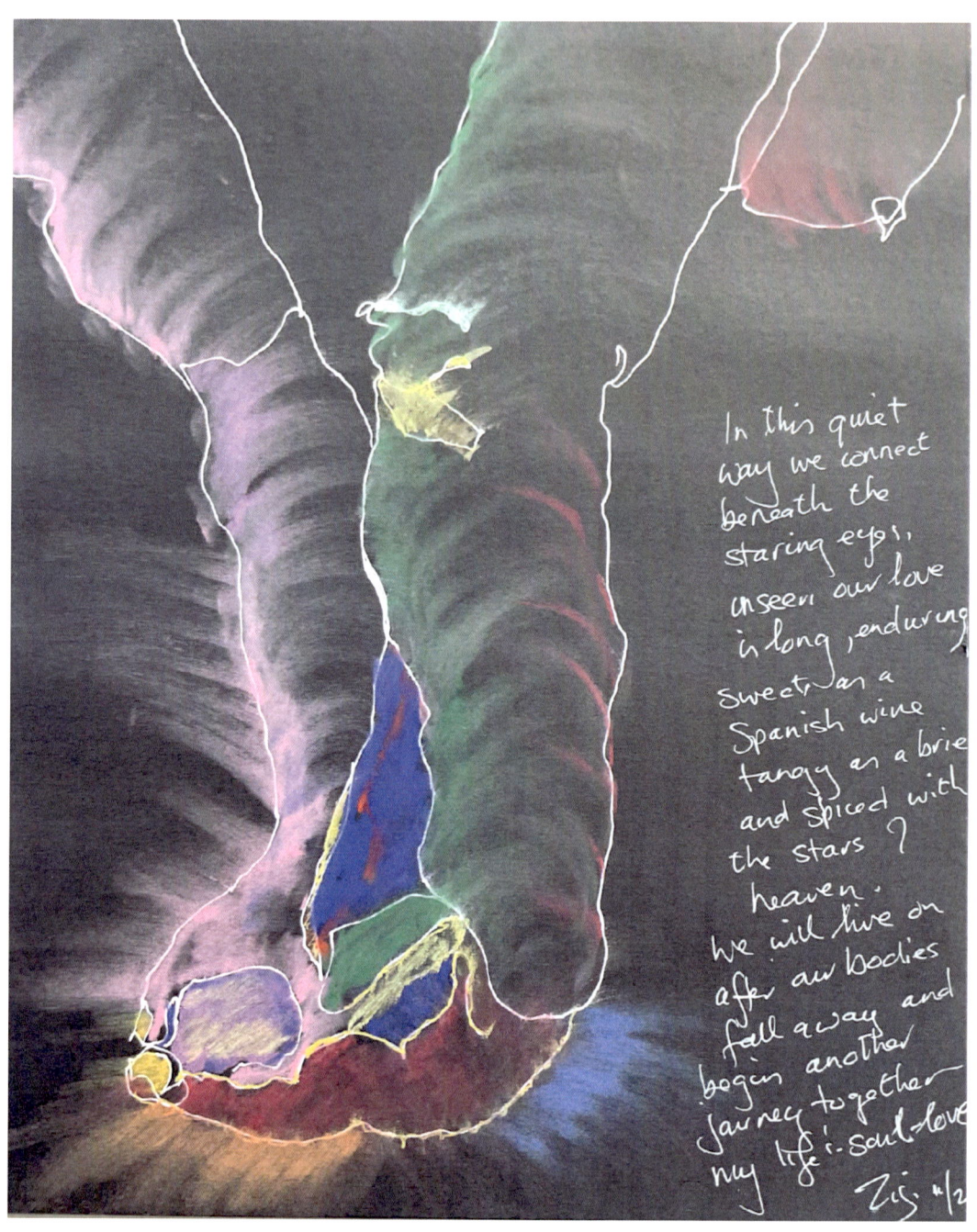

Bound together with Mary Endnote #19

*in this quiet
way we connect
beneath the
star-ring eyes,
unseen our love
is long, enduring
sweet as a
Spanish wine
tangy as a brie
and spiced with
the stars of
heaven.
We will live on
after our bodies
fall away and
begin another
journey together
my life's-soul-love
Ziji 11/22*

Birth 1. #20

I was conceived two months after they buried the kids, while she and her body grieved. Mum must have wondered as do I about the vitality of inbred children. They may have been killed by an outbreak of equine encephalitis. Dad believed the encephalitis was caused by drinking unpasteurised milk on a farm stay holiday.

My parents relocated to South Devon, meeting up again with my future foster mother who was also pregnant at the time. They lived within walking distance of each other. They were to be best friends.

It was here in Devon that my mother went two weeks overdue. Both her previous live births were by caesarean section. I too was born by emergency caesarean. She died giving birth to me. My father didn't attend the funeral. My maternal Grandparents did, and they buried her in the same grave as my brother and sister.

Dad went on an insane road trip on his motorbike to Edinburgh. Grief, guilt, shame and that first betrayal haunted him, and death was on his mind. I remained alone in the neonatal ward for some weeks, unbonded, waiting for my mother to come back to life.

Prayer #21

*take this with you
wherever you go
whichever wind carries you
whoever sings-flies,
you are ageless fragrance
aromas of past and future
gardens made with love
at the birth and twilight
of time
Ziji '21*

Artist diary #22

> *There is a deep pleasure*
> *in waiting for you*
> *and yet like a child in*
> *hospital*
> *the ministrations of nurse*
> *substitutes only touches*
> *the surface*
> *how do I access this deeper*
> *need*
> *this home*
> *when my impulses battle*
> *it out inside*
> *angry that you're*
> *not*
> *here.*

In the complete breakdown of my family that followed, Dad inaccessible, my grandparents' traumatic grief from the loss of two grandchildren and a daughter all within 12 months - Betty and my foster father Norman agreed to look after me for six months.

The pregnancy Betty carried beside my mother's, delivered Julian three months before I was born. He had spina bifida. The hospital practice in those days was not to save spina bifida kids if they were too disabled and likely to be significantly disabled. This was 1949.

Yet it still shocks me to recall, writing these words close to my seventy-fifth birthday, that my foster mother, a GP by profession and likely influenced by the medical beliefs of the time, left her baby in the hospital, and walked away. All the specialists and advisors told her there was no point in keeping him. They must have withdrawn all life support until he passed.

I asked Betty her years later what had happened to Julian. She didn't know but she said it was likely he was incinerated with the hospital waste.

As far as I can remember she had not held the baby nor held a memorial service for him. Standard practice in 1949. Decades later the wife of my youngest foster brother, Jane, miscarried a baby. True to her nature she wanted to hold a memorial service for the child back in the U.K. Betty warmed to the idea and so they held a service for both. This allowed Betty to finally grieve Julian.

In my couple therapy practice I have worked with several lovers who have experienced miscarriages and still births. Their stories are excruciating to hear, and the traumatic load lives on when it was handled badly. Here in 2024, with an excellent health system and considerable understanding of traumatic grief, the tragedy remains in some places a taboo to talk about. This is particularly the case when the child was lost before the 3rd trimester, when most of us tell our family and friends we are pregnant.

In my and Mary's time, we had a few miscarriages early in our pregnancies. In each case we felt the child's presence before they left, as a glowing vibrant energy.

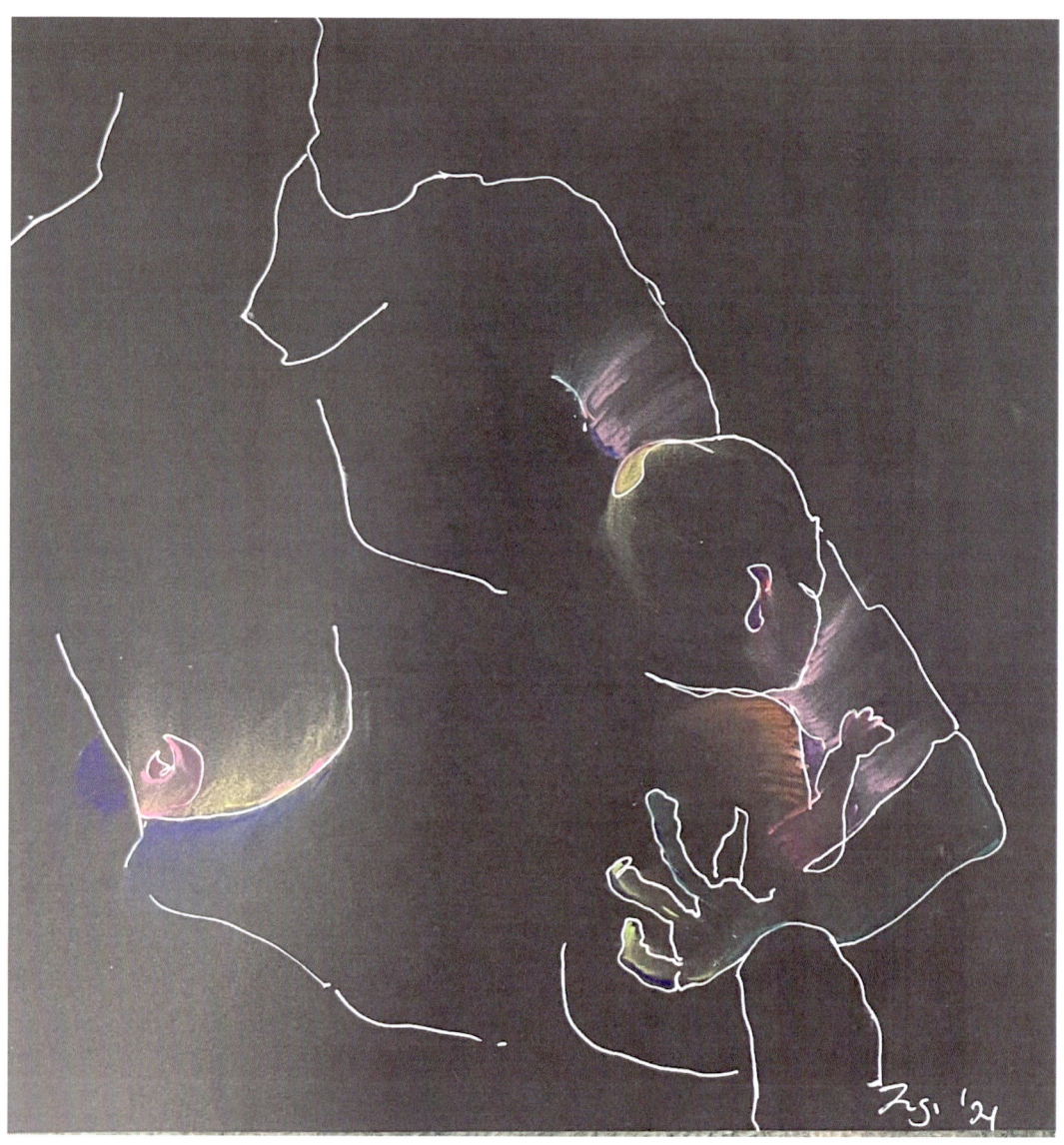

Blessings #23

Ink & wash #24

> taken in whole or in
> part I am too much for
> you, even as entree or
> desert alone, you will
> indigest me. I am more
> than your eye can see, your
> mouth can hold.
> I am me
> Ziji '21

Betty was conceived by unmarried parents, whose families disowned them as a result. They both died when Betty was a teenager. She was an orphan at fourteen years of age. With her spina bifida son recently abandoned and in the depths of grief, I came on the scene, an orphan as well. Her prayers were answered. "Little Peter" was a miracle from God, she told me. All the clothing and bedding that was meant for Julian, was now given to me.

I became the middle blonde child in between two dark-headed brothers. I received plenty of attention while my new parents received kudos for their charity. I lived a wonderful life for eight years. I was a spoiled miracle survivor, with a prayer every night for my mother and a picture of a guardian angel beside my bed.

My favourite person back then was my foster father. A Country GP's practice in Devon before the NHS, was much like the 1978 television series "All Creatures Great and Small". Dad would go on home visits on the weekend, and I would beg to come along. Eager, I would jump in the car with him, my notebook in hand, pretending to be a little medical practitioner.

We'd drive along the narrow country lanes, lined with hedgerows, eventually arriving at a fishing village or a small farm. The farmer's wife would come out to greet us, calling to me to come in, announcing that she'd just pulled a batch of scones out of the oven. Sometimes a fruit cake. She had made clotted cream from last night's milking, and homemade jam.

Dad would begin his checks on each family member: grandpa, mum, dad, children, grandchildren. And, just as we were about to leave, they'd call him back and ask if he could check over the sheepdog or the house cow. Each visit was a two- or three-hour event, and I sat in on it all. Later my foster sister, who was born 4 months after I left the UK, continued the tradition.

Norman had a surgery at home where I would sit in the waiting room and chat to his patients. I loved it. I was being prepped to follow in his footsteps.

I had found myself smack-bang in the middle of a very British, upper middle-class family. On Boxing Day, close servants were invited home for Turkey sandwiches. Lesser persons were given turkey soup the following day. All were so grateful to be part of the annual Christmas ritual. Norman's car was washed every Saturday by the son of his first car washer. That son and probably his father, owned the Rover dealership in Highweek, from whom Dad purchased a new car every couple of years.

From the outside it appeared ideal. However, there was much that was unspoken. My foster mother's regular migraines masked a deep brokenness, maintaining the pretence that everything was normal when she was well. With a migraine, her bedroom curtain was drawn, silence rained, and we kids were on rations. Norman administered pethidine, as required.

She had minimised a career in medicine to support his, and to be a full-time mum. She would have been one of very few women to become a medical practitioner in that era. Later when freed of that duty, she worked as a visiting GP, already dependent on the pethidine that Dad or she prescribed for her migraines. Later she was put on the medical register and obliged to attend a drug rehab program in Exeter. She expressed deep shame about this to me, and yet hid it from her grown up children.

In all the Christian sweetness and light. Anglican Church services every Sunday, the sound of traditional church bellringing (known as change ringing) welcoming us to prayer and driving out the demons. At the conclusion more glorious bells sending us on our way to the much-anticipated family lunch. I was the cuckoo who would later be chucked out of the nest. Character building like British boarding schools. I was grateful to be saved from that fate.

After the informal fostering arrangements were agreed, my biological father absconded, relocating to Western Australia, where he bought an orange orchard in Nedlands. 6 months grew to 8 years. That should have been a red flag to my foster parents.

In that time, Dad had been unable to remarry. He was lonely. He suffered from traumatic grief, chronic anxiety, and morbid fears.

After seven years living in Australia, maintaining only a correspondence with my fosters without returning to the UK, he declared he was now ready to look after me.

This was not in the best interest of any child.[11] Had the arrangements been supervised by U.K. child welfare, they likely would have wanted a fitness to parent report from Australia. The guy should also have been subjected to a psychiatric examination. And then invited to return to the U.K. to build a relationship with me, or not. That didn't happen. The infamous U.K. child migration scheme [12] from 1869 to 1970 exhibited the same failures with far worse results than befell me.

Believing I was too young to travel on my own, and without his willingness to fly home and collect me, they insisted he wait. Aged eight, my foster parents prepared me to travel to Australia to live with a stranger, a broken man. My foster mother was 4 months pregnant with twins.

The Australian Government paid for my ticket. I was a 'ten-pound pom'[13] like Prime Minister Julia Gillard, who bless her, set up the Child Abuse Royal Commission that pursued my case.[14]

On a visit to the UK in 2023 my foster niece apologised on behalf of her grandparents for a decision that in hindsight was reckless. It opened the door to abuse. That outcome was unthinkable then. Jimmy Saville [15] was nowhere on the horizon.[16]

Their good deed of fostering me did not go unpunished.[17]

---

[11] UN Convention on the Rights of the Child 1990. These principles applied in the UK and Australia in the 1950's. The UN Charter formalised those principles. As a country we were and still are so far from this. We detain child refugees and The Stolen Generation continue in another form.

https://en.wikipedia.org/wiki/Convention_on_the_Rights_of_the_Child

[12] https://en.wikipedia.org/wiki/Home_Children

[13] https://en.wikipedia.org/wiki/Ten_Pound_Poms

[14] 'We know from what victims and survivors tell us that being able to report what happened to the police is healing for many people, sometimes even when a case cannot be pursued.' https://en.wikipedia.org/wiki/Operation_Hydrant

[15] https://en.wikipedia.org/wiki/Jimmy_Savile_sexual_abuse_scandal

[16] https://en.wikipedia.org/wiki/Operation_Hydrant

[17] A virtuous deed turns into a curse, good actions bring forth adversity.

Loss #25

> we are part of every sunset
> and each insect in flight
> and all the palm and ferns
> but leaves of life swollen
> with joy and gratitude.
> take me with you when you
> fly and be with me when I
> die.
> Ziji

V2P again #26

*Our time slips so easily
like clouds rising in the valley
we breathe and are touched
beauty all around
jasmine flowering
wild in the forest
lost in the dream
life slips by
and the magpie
still asks for food
knocks my coffee
on the park bench
not troubled by
our grief
for a moment
when a voice
might be heard*

Ziji 18/10/23

MEETING THE FATHER #27

My eighteen-year-old cousin Patricia was my caretaker on the flight and for the first 6 months my au pair in Australia. Her widower father Joe Fox was Chaplain of HM Prison Dartmoor. She couldn't escape the bitterly cold, grey granite home in the prison grounds fast enough, and jumped at the opportunity to travel with me. It was an hilarious trip, her flirting with the Australia Cricket team on board. It was a grown-up party like I had never experienced.

We landed at Tullamarine Airport and there, across the tarmac, was a faceless shell of a man standing next to a black FJ Holden.

He resembled the photograph I had of my father. Excited, I climbed down the stairs from the Qantas Super Constellation and ran at him like a freight train. I leapt into his arms, expecting to be held by my dad. But he was completely frozen. He had no idea how to deal with such a force of nature.

It was clear that my new life in Australia had gained me incredible freedom. The sky was always blue, I was free to speak about anything. I had a single father who had only me as his object of attention. We lived in Beaumaris, at the edge of the beach in Melbourne where I could ride my bike on the sand hills, smoke cigarettes in my tree house, eat whatever I liked whenever I liked. I even had a dog! I knew I was lucky in so many ways and from the outside I appeared happy.

However, I was in survival mode using the social engagement strategy of trauma called 'fawning'. It is a response to threat by becoming more appealing. It is my strategy of scanning people, situations and places and using that information to decide where I might exert influence. On the outside, I became whatever care givers wanted me to be, to get my needs met, whilst I remained hidden inside. Isolated, alone, needy and as some friends of dad's observed insecure with an air of tragedy about me. The body never lies but I don't remember ever feeling my insides. I was numb to the inner life that I wore on my skin.

The following poem speaks to the gift of that strategy. Like a chameleon, I could be whatever was needed to stay hidden and yet be of service to another's need for connection.

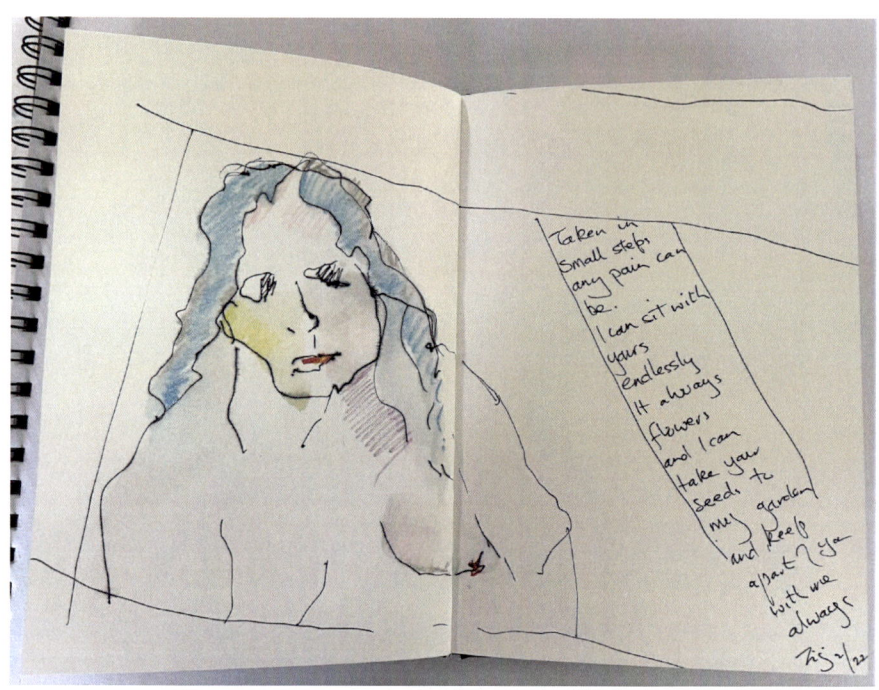

Love song #28

*Taken in
small steps
any pain can
be.
I can sit with
yours
endlessly
it always
flowers
and I can
take your
seeds to
my garden
and keep
a part of you
with me
always
Ziji 2/22*

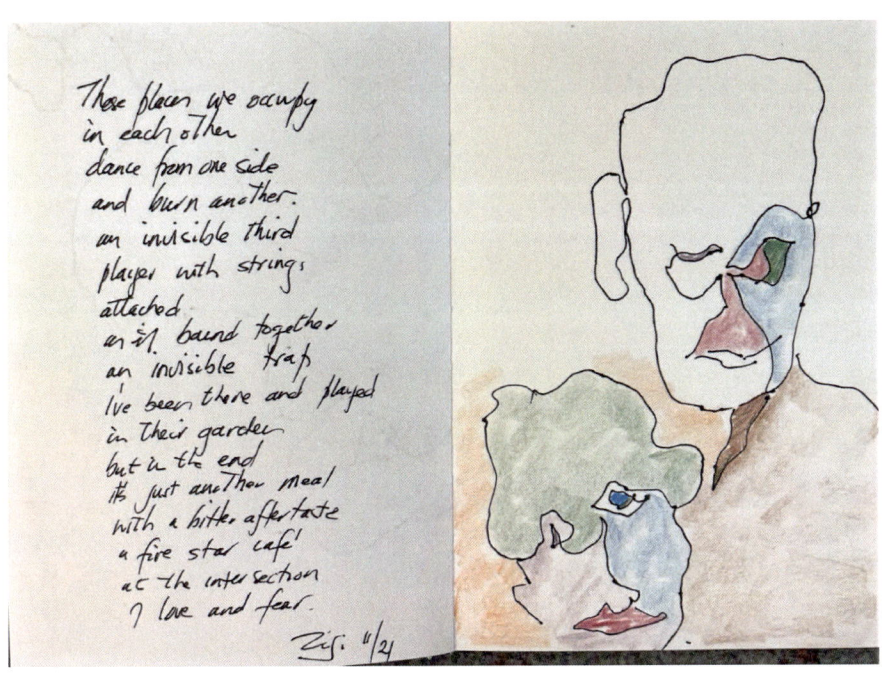

Immersion #29

> *These places we occupy*
> *in each other*
> *dance from one side*
> *and burn another.*
> *An invisible third*
> *player with strings*
> *attached*
> *as if bound together*
> *an invisible trap*
> *I've been there and played*
> *in their garden*
> *but in the end*
> *it's just another meal*
> *with a bitter aftertaste*
> *a five-star café*
> *at the intersection*
> *of love and fear*
> *Ziji 11/21*

Work inspires #30

Maybe those sad eyes will
draw another landscape
but the rest of you
tears at the bond of intimacy
we build each day.
Can you ever leave that behind
and just be in the joy of the present?
Ziji 2/22

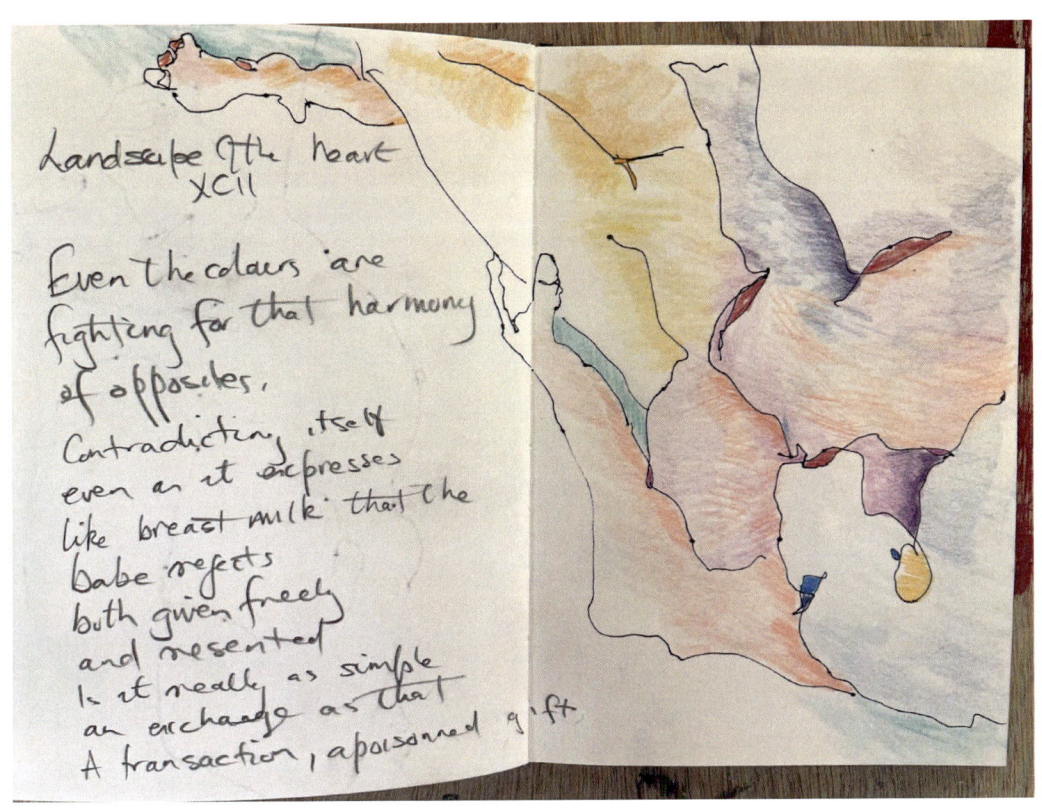

Paired #31

Landscape of the heart xcii
Even the colours are
fighting for that harmony
of opposites.
Contradicting itself
even as it expresses
like breast milk that the
babe rejects
both given freely
and resented.
Is it really as simple
an exchange as that?
A transaction, a poisoned gift?

Over time, I called him 'dear-old-dad-who-is-so-mad'. I wrote on my bedroom wall 'I hate dad, I love dad'. I went to my first child psychologist in Beaumaris age 9. At some level I realised, I was going to have to be his caretaker. I became a parentified child and resented it.

I started smoking cigarettes. I bought my first packet of Lucky Strike from the local shop, with a packet of lollies or a Fanta.

A decade later it would be Gauloise and Sobranie. I sat in the University of NSW coffee shop reading the International Herald Tribune with a cappuccino, smoking a Black Russian.

It was one of many attempts putting on a front as a means of survival. A projection of many selves. Pretending everything was normal as my foster mother had taught me.

Here's a self-portrait of these selves without a poem. A map of Australia in the mouth, absent Tasmania, and fearful eyes looking away from the present. The colours and mark making speak of energetic confusion, survival shape shifting.

Shouldered on a grey body; mark making like gusts of rain falling and reprised in the top of the mostly left brain are grey sparks, suggesting aliveness and perhaps numb body experience. And all that sea blue reaching from mouth, down the throat into the heart – the unspoken that might later infuse the body with sense memory and a name. That's my take on it. I made the image in about 15 minutes without planning or thinking.

I look at that today, 2 years after it emerged from the back of my mind, and there I am! I have a chip on my right shoulder and an orange osteoarthritic inflammation on the left side of my neck. Both true. I learnt the Metamorphic Technique decades ago from Gaston St Pierre.[18] He could read the whole of a life just from the feet. My feet would tell the same story today as this self-portrait. And yet I experience myself as whole and unbroken, well, most of the time I do. My art/poems reveal another story.

---

[18] https://www.metamorphicassociation.org/en/general-information/founder/

ADELAIDE

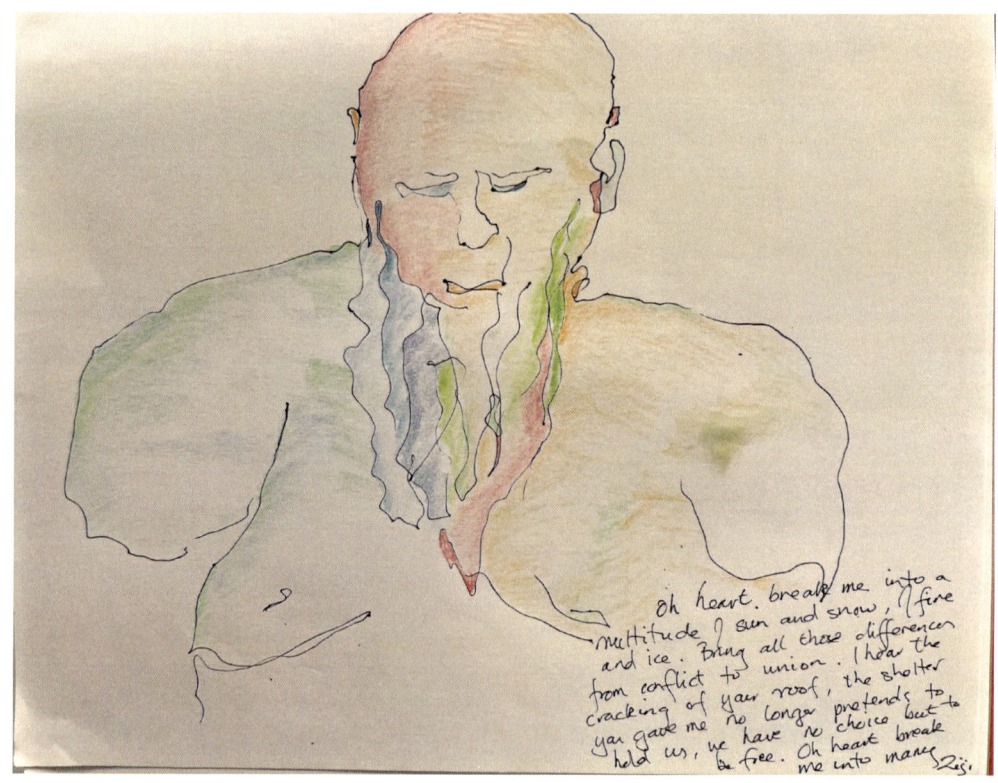

oh heart, break me into a
multitude of sun and snow, of fire
and ice. Bring all these differences
from conflict to union. I hear the
cracking of your roof, the shelter
you gave me no longer pretends to
hold us, we have no choice but to
be free. Oh heart break
me into many
Ziji

My father was insecure and anxious. Work environments and people became problematic for him. As a result, we moved cities a lot. He was always looking for the greener grass. We moved from Melbourne to Adelaide. More upheaval.

My father's sister Delie had emigrated from the UK to Perth to be near dad. Then, when he moved from Perth via Melbourne to Adelaide, she moved again to South Australia to be near him, hoping to make a normal family with two boys, a mother figure, and a father figure. My father and his sister were also cousins.

Her only son was born with spina bifida. My aunt *refused* to listen to the experts. She had lost her husband, his father, in a military accident before he was born. She fought for the kid and eventually gained his release from hospital. She chased down every avenue of help for him, encouraged him to enter sports, ride horses, and he ended up being a wonderful guy and later a mate to me.

When my aunt arrived in Adelaide to join us, it felt at last like I had a family again. She bought an orchard in the Adelaide hills. Wine country. One of dad's work colleagues owned a rose farm nearby. They distilled rose essence, rose wine, made chocolates, and drove a Fiat Bambino down a winding road to the city. So many sensory delights!

The next image, page 58, reminds me of the archetype of the Hangman in the Tarot. It has been years since I used a Tarot pack in my personal and professional life, yet here it is re-appearing in this piece.

To me the Hangman is about the presence of the shadow self's influence in my nervous system's reactions to current events. It is about choosing to surrender to life rather than take action to avoid it. The poem speaks to the uncertainty of what the future holds 'will I be okay' whilst fearing the past of broken dreams and fearing those losses will recur. Should I take that step or as the Hangman suggests, take no action, and allow the universe to work without my interference. I hadn't considered the significance of this piece until putting this book together a year or so after drawing it.

> if I take th……is step
> toward you……..will I be okay?
> do I believe………you? so many
> broken cities………..of dreams
> is this one…………another promised
> loss?

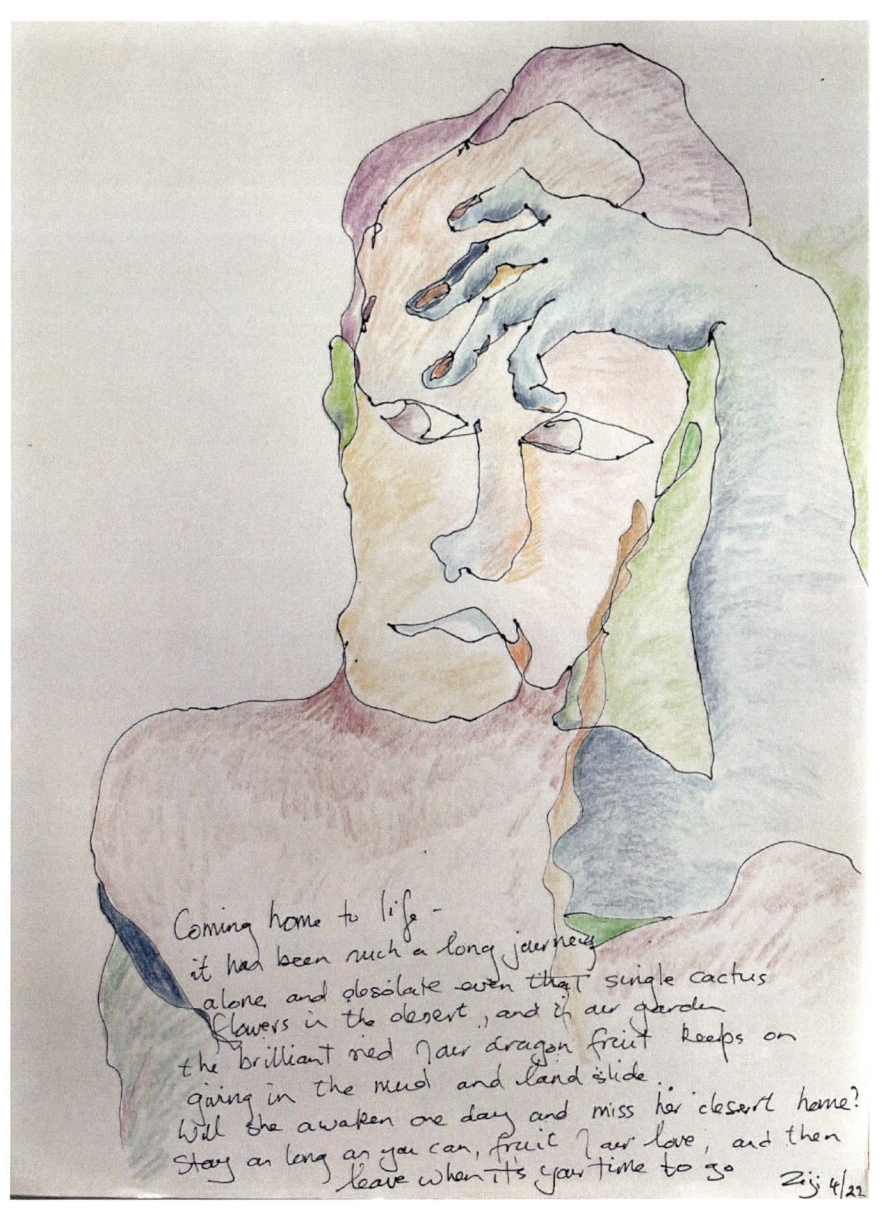

Coming home to life -
it has been such a long journey
alone and desolate even that single cactus
flowers in the desert, and in our garden
the brilliant red of our dragon fruit keeps on
giving in the mud and the landslide.
Will she awaken one day and miss her desert home?
Stay as long as you can, fruit of our love, and then
leave when it's your time to go.
Ziji 4/22

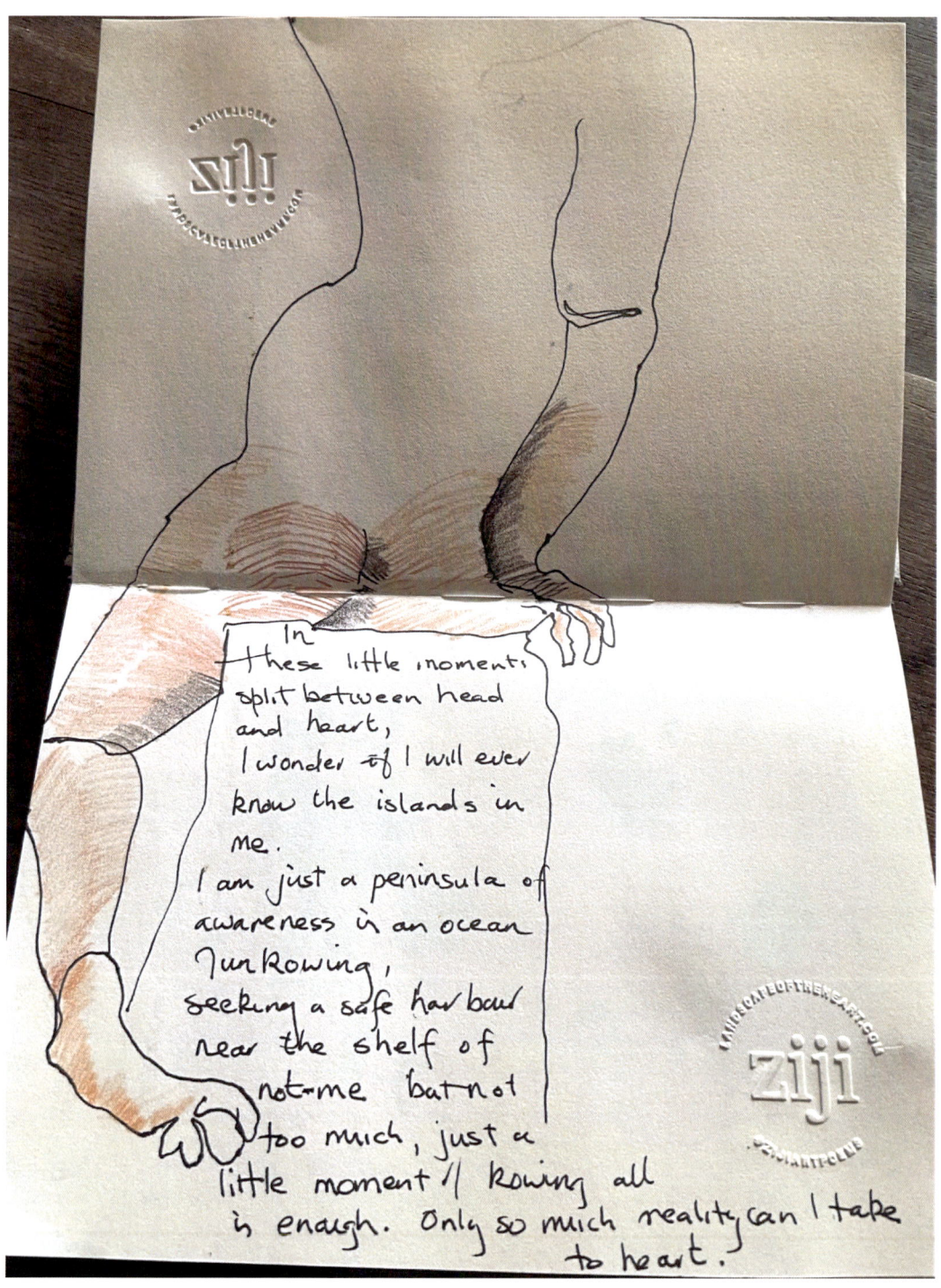

In these little moments split between head and heart, I wonder if I will ever know the islands in me.
I am just a peninsula of awareness in an ocean Junkowing, seeking a safe harbour near the shelf of not-me but not too much, just a little moment // knowing all is enough. Only so much reality can I take to heart.

*In
these little moments
split between head
and heart,
I wonder if I will ever
know the islands in
me.
I am just a peninsula of
awareness in an ocean
of unknowing,
seeking a safe harbour
near the shelf of
not-me but not
too much, just
a little moment of knowing all
is enough. only so much reality can I take
to heart.*

I went to Scots College in Adelaide, where the principal encouraged dad to let me board so he would have some respite. For one term as a border, I felt part of a community, a member of a group of good people who cared for me, but dad couldn't live without me. So, I had to return to home.

There my aunt continued to love me in many ways. She made me food to take home, did my laundry and ironed my hankies. She sang old folk songs and drank a nip or two before bed. Talked with me about this difficult man, her brother. I would spend time in her orchard where my cousin drove me around in his Land Rover until I was confident to do it myself at age twelve. Things felt easy.

But my dad couldn't tolerate my being close to anyone else. He feared losing me. He was jealous and possessive in a toxic way.

And I could never give him what he wanted, which was my affection. From my perspective, he had stolen me from my family, stolen my life. I hated him and loved him. I was chronically unwell. Dad made the next move. This time to Tasmania.

I have written about this time in Tasmania, both in this art/poetry book, and at length in my autobiographical novel, 'The Dream Life of Debris 2nd Edition'. Some sequences in that book occurred, but the rest is a fictionalised download of much that I have learnt about the dynamics of relationships. The paedophile character is drawn from a client who was mandated for treatment after early release from jail. He had been tried and convicted of those offenses.

I found it gut wrenching and healing to write 'Dream Life'. I love the sense of triumph I experienced in putting it down on paper. What follows is the real stuff. Though I acknowledge from a post-structuralist [19] narrative point of view, and from the research of cognitive science, any experience told more than twice increasingly becomes fiction. It was only through the Child Abuse Royal Commission procedures that I took in the fact that I was both a witness and a victim.[20] I had previously thought that without corroboration the fact of abuse could not be proved.

---

[19] https://www-archiv.fdm.uni-hamburg.de/lhn/node/56.html

[20] https://www.childabuseroyalcommission.gov.au/identifying-and-disclosing-child-sexual-abuse

Travellers #32

> *We travel so far on land*
> *yet stay in one pace in our hearts.*
> *It wouldn't matter where the wind*
> *blows us, I will always find you*
> *there, singing old folk songs*
> *and drinking rye.*
> *So, take me there one more time*
> *before I go.*
> *You make my world a travel diary*
> *Ziji 12/22*
> *saskia*

HOBART

HEALTH WARNING: THIS IS A SECTION ABOUT ABUSE! TRAUMA TRIGGERS AHEAD!!

We had no one in Hobart. Not friends nor family. No work colleagues to fill the gap as Dad had in Melbourne and Adelaide.

For the first couple of weeks, we lived in a caravan park before eventually moving into a flat on Molle Street near the school I would soon attend: The Hutchins School. It was here, amongst the English-looking limestone buildings, that I was introduced to the headmaster, David Lawrence.[21] I didn't realise at the time how important he would become in my life.

David was the only person that really looked after me in Tasmania. Kind, warm, and seemingly very interested in me, he encouraged me to do cross country and made sure I was in the right classes. He made sure none of the other paedophiles in the school came near.

I was his bitch.

He reminded me of my foster father. The same aftershave. The same soft hands. Fragmented memories of home. The Oxbridge English accent. On one hand, he protected me and on the other, he sexually violated me. It was a perfect combination: I was a vulnerable, lost, isolated, frightened teenage boy and he was a serial, 'career' paedophile who knew exactly what he was doing.

I wrote 'Dream Life of Debris 2nd Edition'[22] as a way of transforming that story as an autobiographical novel.[23]

---

[21] https://www.abc.net.au/news/2014-11-19/sexual-abuse-by-hutchins-school-staff-widely-known-inquiry-told/5901906/

[22] ISBN 9780645967210

[23] https://en.wikipedia.org/wiki/Autobiographical_novel

Breathe #33

> *There are places in here we hardly*
> *know, until*
> *in a brief slice in the fabric of time*
> *on a lonely road*
> *one speaks to us, from a time*
> *long forgotten; we are*
> *just held in a fragment of memory*
> *long enough to know our source,*
> *the fruit of many lives,*
> *and one speaks to us*
> *'it's going to be okay*
> *you are in a sea of wellness'*
> *just rest here and breathe*
> *for a moment of time*
> *Ziji 7/22*

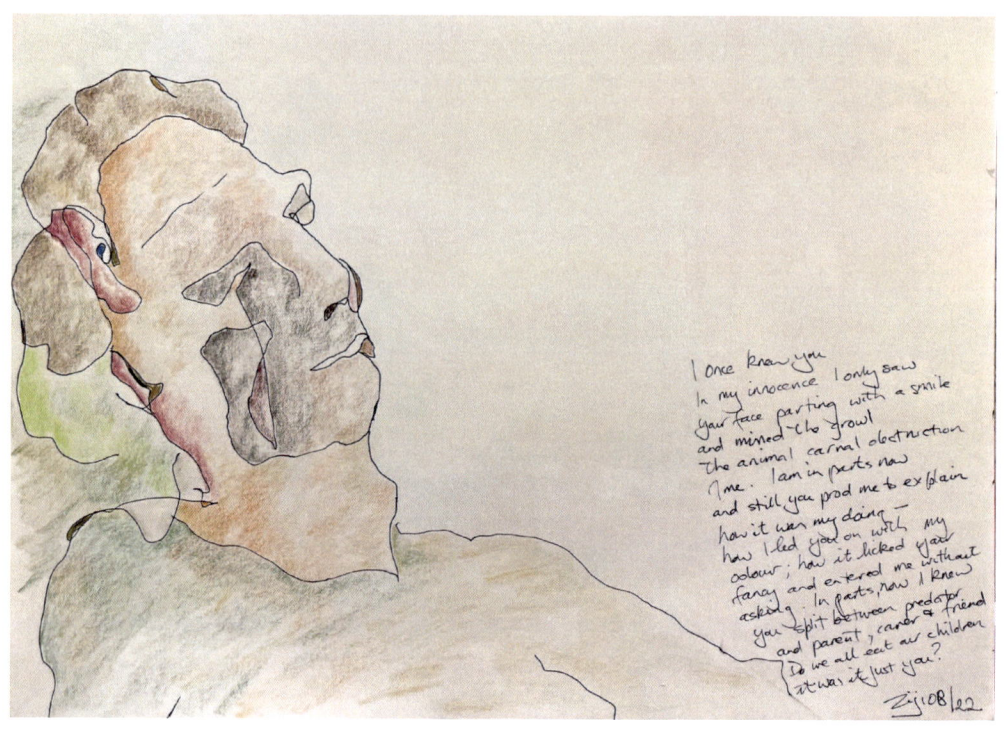

A first #34

> *I once knew you.*
> *in my innocence I only saw*
> *your face parting with a smile*
> *and missed the growl*
> *the animal carnal destruction*
> *of me. I am in parts now*
> *and still you prod me to explain*
> *how was it my doing –*
> *how I led you on with my*
> *odour; how it licked your*
> *fancy and entered me without*
> *asking. In parts, now I know*
> *you split between predator*
> *and parent, carer & friend.*
> *Do we all eat out children*
> *or was it just you?*
> *Ziji 18/08/22*

It went on for a whole year.

Eventually, the same old pattern arose of dad being jealous of the other. But this time it saved my life and interrupted the grooming to enlist me as a procurer. When dad announced we were leaving Hobart, I was more furious with him than ever. He was taking me away from David. I didn't know it was wrong. I didn't know it was abuse. I just knew it was a deal: if you want to have special attention from the headmaster, you give him sex.

The first headmaster of the Hutchins School that I disclosed the abuse to, after investigating the case he told me Lawrence loved me.

Subsequent headmasters and successive school boards continued that falsehood for more than twenty years as I worked to be heard, the damage respected and acknowledged, and to be cared for by the school. I enlisted the help of two Bishops of Tasmania, to no avail.

Later, in the Child Abuse Royal Commission Public Hearing 20, where I gave my testimony, we discovered there were about six paedophiles working at the school at the same time as Lawrence.

When I first disclosed my story to the school in my early forties, the school claimed there were no paedophiles there. No victims even though I was declaring myself to be one. We're terribly sorry, they wrote on one occasion, but' we're not accountable for the actions of a previous generation'.

This was finally resolved in 2022, sixty years after the abuse began.

David Lawrence had come to Tasmania from Canterbury Cathedral where he was choirmaster and organist. He was a career paedophile. He practiced a venomous even lethal skill with impunity. He had trained himself or had been trained, to offer vulnerable victims what they needed.

When I was ready to bring it to the surface with Saskia, I asked her to adopt a vulnerable pose that I hoped would provoke these memories. I have written about this method in the Appendix.

I will let the following images speak for themselves.

*And there, just on the edge of
consciousness, asleep, you creep
toward me, take what you want
and leave me in pieces.
Ziji   09/02/23*

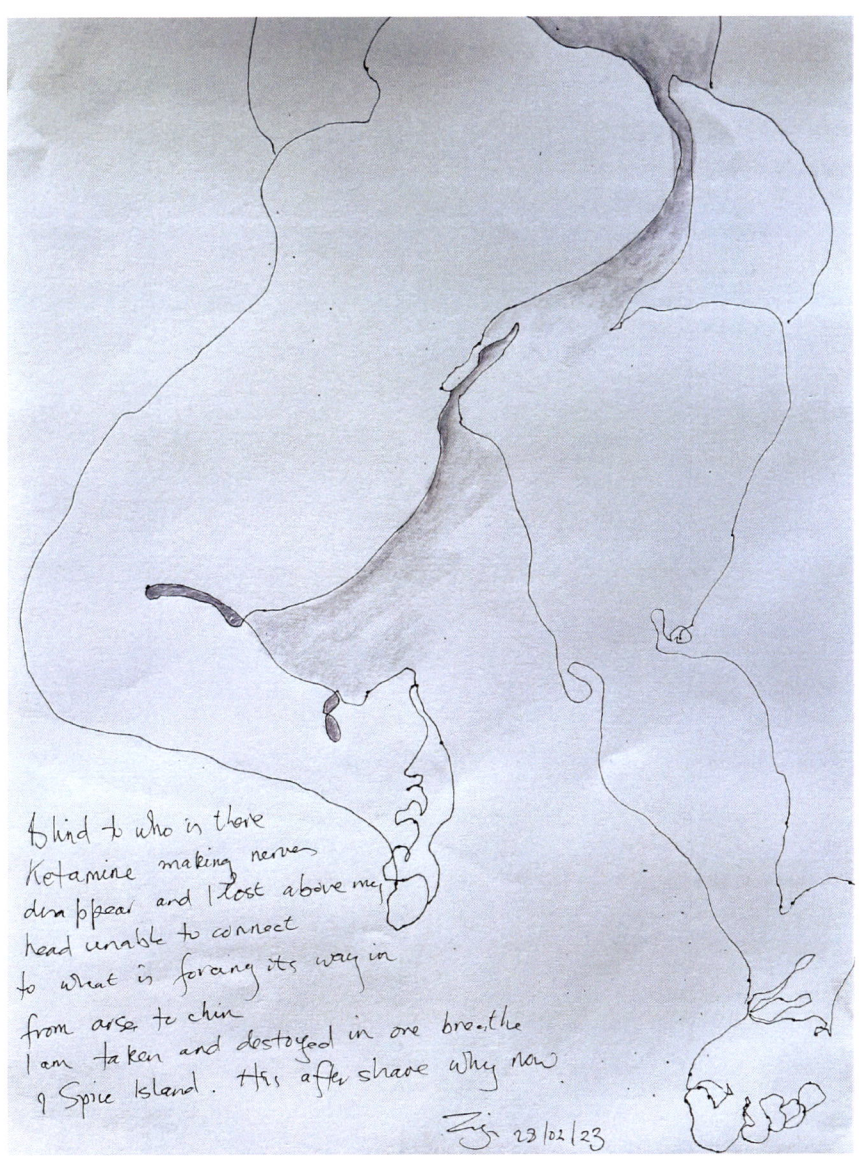

Blind to who is there
ketamine making nerves
disappear and I lost above my
head unable to connect
to what is forcing its way in
from arse to chin
I am taken and destroyed in one breath
of spice island. His after shave why now.
Ziji 28/02/23

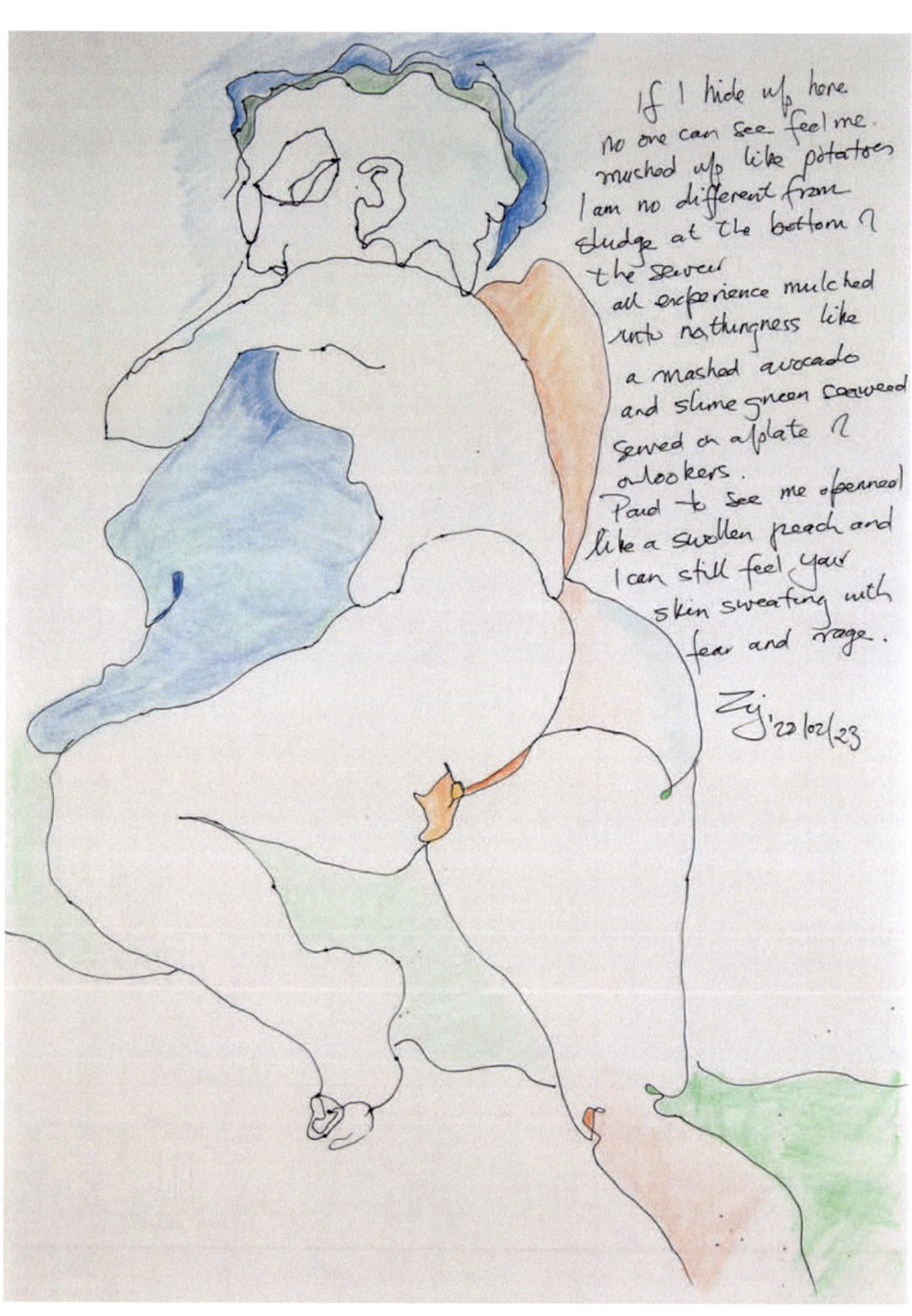

*If I hide up here
no one can see feel me
mashed up like potatoes
I am no different from
sludge at the bottom of
the sewer
all experience mulched
into nothingness like
a mashed avocado
and slime green seaweed
served on a plate of
onlookers.
paid to see me opened
like a swollen peach and
I can still feel your skin sweating with
fear and rage.
Ziji 28/02/23*

When I review my experience as a victim, I understand it was systemic grooming.[24] It was an institution complicit malevolence. Lawrence didn't just groom me. He emotionally seduced my father; the deputy head; the Chaplain; the school secretary; the school board, and the parents.[25] How did he persuade that young policeman (who came to question him about a complaint of sex abuse) and his senior officer, to come back in two weeks with an arrest warrant? [26] He used the time to return to the UK without facing the consequences of his crimes.

[24] https://en.wikipedia.org/wiki/Sexual_grooming

https://www.childsafety.gov.au/about-child-sexual-abuse/grooming/

[25] https://pureadmin.qub.ac.uk/ws/portalfiles/portal/140510907/3_Savile_Chapter_McAlinden_Final.pdf

[26] Evidence presented at Child Abuse Royal Commission Case 20.

NORTH

We left Hobart after twelve months, and travelled north, to Cooma, NSW sheep country. Along the way we camped along the Great Ocean Road. One evening, dad asked me to help him put up the tent, but I stormed off, furious with him for taking me away from David.

Aged fourteen, I walked to the edge of the Great Ocean Road and looked straight down. I closed my eyes and imagined the whole process: jumping, falling, landing and my body splattered all over the rocks. I saw the whole thing in technicolour. I imagined dad seeing me on the rocks below, feeling terrible and deeply remorseful. I wanted him to feel as terrible as I was feeling.

I pulled back from the edge determined to make his life hell. I needed to dig two graves for that mission. I was now clinically depressed and with complex traumatic grief. At the time there was no real language for this wounding. At 14 years of age, the brain is still developing. I liken the experience to an acquired brain injury, manifesting in changes in my brain's structure and functioning.[27] In fact most trauma survivors recover naturally.[28] I didn't.

In Cooma, we stayed with a wealthy pastoral family, friends of dad from our holidays in Gippsland, Victoria. Mahogany tables, silver candelabras, vases of fresh flowers formally laid out, servants. We dressed formally for dinners. Children were seen, not heard. It was a whole other world to me.

One morning we went out shooting kangaroos for dog food. I had my own 0.22-gauge rifle. We all hid behind the rocks, and one of the men on horseback chased the 'roos so they'd run past the rocks where we could shoot them. Clay pigeon mentality. Technically, it would be cheaper and more energy efficient to buy the meat, but the process was about status. It was 'what you did'.

That evening at dinner, something dad said just set me off and, in my rage, I swore at him. The lady of the house took offence to a child speaking to an adult like that, and forcibly sent me to my

---

[27] https://www.ncbi.nlm.nih.gov/pmc/articles/PMC2729089/

[28] https://www.nature.com/articles/s41398-021-01633-y

room. I felt humiliated, ashamed, and betrayed by dad. In that moment he didn't have my back. He was a weak man with a broken heart and so much unresolved trauma from his family and the war.

I stormed off to my bedroom, closed the door, got out Dad's .303 and loaded it. It was a beautiful sniper's rifle from WWII. I sat on the edge of the bed waiting to shoot the bastard when he walked through the door. But no one came. Eventually I fell asleep.

Dad must have found me asleep, loaded gun beside me. When I woke up in the morning I was tucked into bed, gun uncocked, unloaded, and neatly put away.

And no one ever spoke a word about it. In retrospect it was the paedophile who should have been eliminated.

#35

#36

*This peace we find
together, slips like the
sea over shells and rocks
wearing away our fright.
This peace we make rubbing against
and with
each other's edges, fills some unfound place
inside. Some place longing for the beloved
found, loved, held, whole, made whole again
through being broken.
This peace comes even to the broken places
inside me, where I long to be held, made whole.
Oh dear ocean keep washing and rubbing
the shells and rock that I filled
in to hide the broken.*

Ziji 7/22

Disembodied May 2022

This self-portrait with the body cut off at the diaphragm was inspired by one of our male models with gorgeous long curling hair, and a black motorbike.

I let the pen go where it wanted and then came back with Derwent colour pencils. Half the face is missing and the left arm like a thalidomide survivor birth defect. The right side of the face (your left) has a clear mouth, nose and eyes looking into the empty left side of the face on your right.

Like one of those optical illusions with an image that is both a vase and two faces, called Rubin's vase.[29]

I have concluded that one way the unconscious has of communicating, is by a visual, auditory even a kinaesthetic illusion. I stop to feel into it and extract personal meaning.

For me this one could be about an imbalance in development - specifically of the left and feminine side of the body, and the left and verbal side of the brain. [30] The receptive side of the body raped and verbal side of the brain unable to speak.

And that interpretation may be an example of pareidolia [31] - imposing a meaning where there is none, particularly on visual objects. My inclination in this book is to impose a right brain metaphorical interpretation on a fuzzy image.

All that aside I love this one's hair and split face and the drift toward abstraction. Kandinsky's path to abstraction [32] has had a strong influence on my courage to let go. I want my work to organically veer toward an abstract languaging of my experience. This next image p.80 speaks to the spiritual in art, where Kandinsky travelled in his own way.

---

[29] https://en.wikipedia.org/wiki/Rubin_vase

[30] 'British psychiatrist Iain McGilchrist ... view(s) the two hemispheres as having different value systems, where the left hemisphere tends to reduce complex matters such as ethics to rules and measures, and the right hemisphere is disposed to the holistic and metaphorical.' https://en.wikipedia.org/wiki/Lateralization_of_brain_function

[31] https://en.wikipedia.org/wiki/Pareidolia

[32] https://www.tate.org.uk/whats-on/tate-modern/kandinsky-path-abstraction

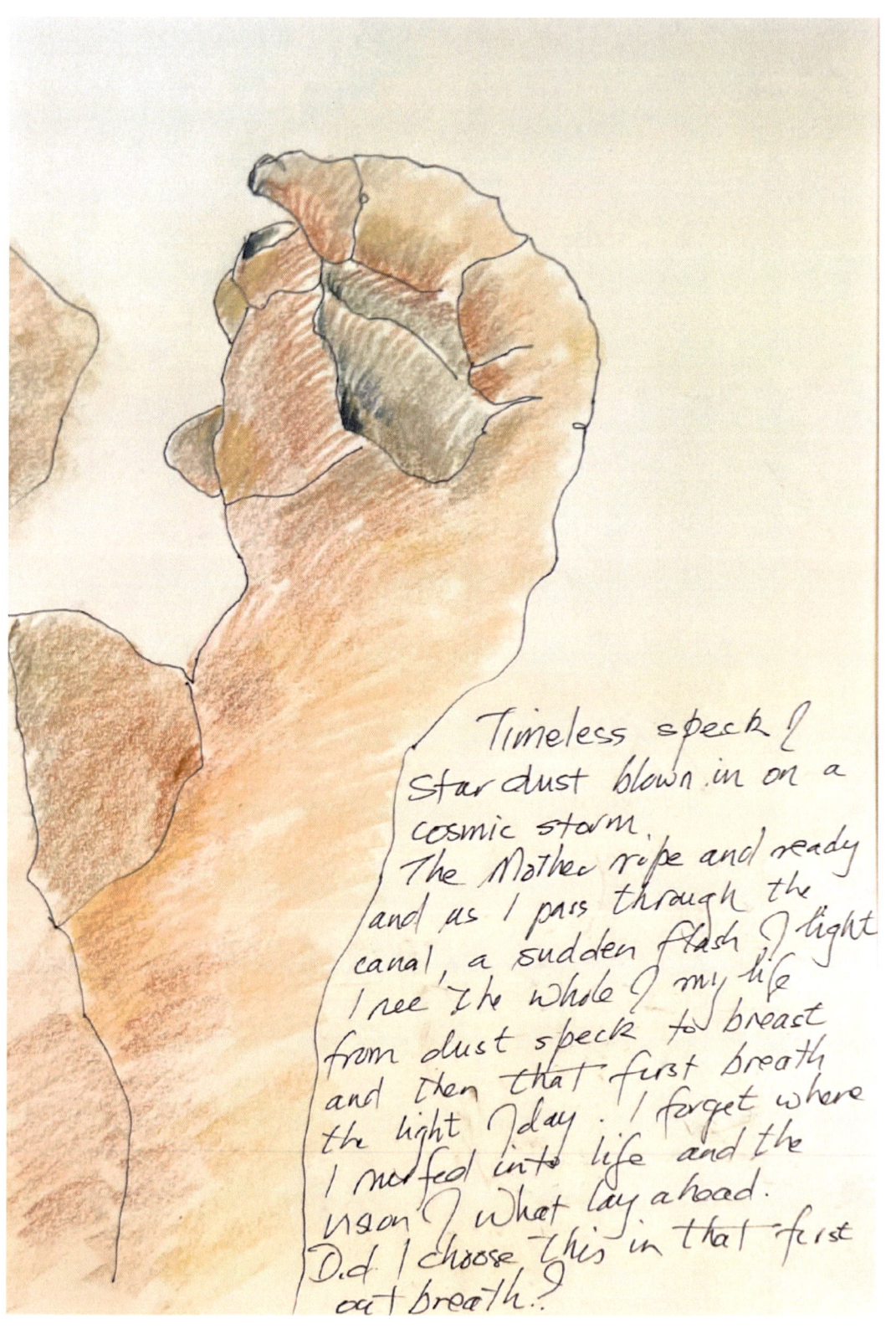

Timeless speck
Star dust blown in on a cosmic storm.
The Mother ripe and ready
and as I pass through the canal, a sudden flash of light
I see the whole of my life
from dust speck to breast
and then that first breath
the light of day. I forget where I merged into life and the vision of what lay ahead.
Did I choose this in that first out breath?

#37

*Timeless speck of
stardust blown in on a
cosmic storm.
The mother ripe and ready
and as I pass through the
canal, a sudden flash of light
I see the whole of my life
from dust speck to breast
and then that first breath
the light of day. I forget where
I surfed into life and the
vision of what lay ahead.
Did I choose this in that first out breath?*

BRISBANE

When we moved to Brisbane, I suffered with constant inflammation and related ill health in my body, mind, and soul. I continued to rage with homicidal thoughts towards my father, and toward myself.

I went to the Church of England Grammar School for Boys (Churchie). I formed a gang with other dropouts and marginalised (mostly gay) people. I never had a sexual relationship with any of them because in my naivety and underlying trauma from what had unfolded at the Hutchins school, I didn't know they were gay. Lawrence was not a homosexual.

My friends and I would smoke and play cards at the back of the sports oval and turn up to class late. Nothing was ever said, and this always amazed me, because I seemed in retrospect, to be a screaming obvious example of a severely traumatised kid. I was underweight, pale, dissociated, inattentive, hypervigilant but no one ever thought to ask me if I was okay. This is late 1960's so no surprise.

One of the kids in my social circle was Ian. He had an arts practice and attended Mervin Moriarty's Flying Art School based in South Brisbane. Mervin would fly to remote aboriginal communities to teach art. It was here that I learned to draw. Mervin's Brisbane-based aboriginal students did startling paintings in screaming colours that clashed up against each other, the edges vibrating.

In class I just drew with a graphite pencil. Apart from doodles, it was the first art thing I ever did. I was seventeen. Broken and suicidal. Their vibrant colours were hope.

Here is a diptych I did in 2006 in Canberra, which celebrates that influence. I eventually worked it into a triptych which lives in our bedroom and brings me joy every morning. From our window below it, we can see the waterfall in the distance, and nearby the rosella's eating the flowers in the tree. In the middle distance the rainforest we are regenerating and the koala corridor we are building. I now live in an artist's and a gardener's paradise.

For the first time, aged 18, I took hold of my broken life. I made a pact with myself to put it all behind me. I would put on another mask and live. I told my father there was no way I was going to finish school.

And so, the dear man that he was at heart, investigated what one does with such a child – and found the Hubbard Academy.

Somewhere in this journey I discovered Martin Buber [33]: *Everyone must come out of his Exile in his own way.*[38] Even today his words below touch my heart.

> *Every person born into the world represents something new, something that never existed before, something original and unique. If there had been someone like her in the world, there would have been no need for her to be born.*
>
> *Every one's foremost task is the actualization of this unique, unprecedented, and never-recurring potentialities, and not the repetition of something that another, and be it even the greatest, has already achieved.*

---

[33] https://en.wikipedia.org/wiki/Martin_Buber

Maybe you can't take this life
turn it around to better fit you
So little change is brought on by
another
We have to find our own way
and recognize the crutches we
use to hold us up
Eventually all palm fronds
and walking stick turn to dust
as do we. So now, take this life
in your own hands and live it fully
We are here so short a time,
I will eat this life like a giant
and leave full filled

Ziji 9/02/23

*Maybe you can't take this life
turn it around to better fit you
so little change is brought on by
another.
We have to find our own way
and recognize the crutches we
use to hold us up.
Eventually all palm fronds
and walking stick turn to dust
as do we. So now, take this life
in your own hands and live it fully
we are here so short a time,
I will eat this life like a giant
and leave full filled.
Ziji 9/02/23*

CO-ED

Hubbard was a co-educational school, unrelated to Scientology's L. Ron Hubbard. It crammed the two final years of school into one. They taught us how to answer the questions in each subject from the last ten years or so of matriculation exams. They based everything on: "how do you answer that question?"

We all wrote learnt a paragraph from the most likely Shakespearean plays. We had a few lines of the most likely Gerard Manley Hopkins poems. We had high points from the history of western civilization. Same with maths and science. And then, after a year of studying, we went to the matriculation exam where we'd write the answer that we had prepared, critiqued, and workshopped. I flew through the exams. I found it extraordinary that I did so well when everything else felt lived under a heavy blanket of what I later understood as depression, hurt and shame.[34]

I was desperately shy around girls. On a zoological excursion to Moreton Bay, I tried to hide my erection; the result of the combination of sitting next to a real-life girl and the bouncing motion of the bus. It was my first experience of heterosexual arousal.

I got into Vet Science because at the time, that's what I thought I wanted to do. The Vet Science crew in Brisbane were a boozy lot. This suited me fine because I was heavily self-medicating. Young and reckless, I managed to get up in the morning to attend lectures. I'd turn up to anatomy class without a clue. I had none of the basic grounding in English, maths, science, or physics. All I knew how to do was to regurgitate what I had read and answer the question in the matriculation. That's all I had.

Vet Science was not for me.

---

[34] I learnt about this from John Bradshaw.

https://www.youtube.com/watch?v=5q2tZa1gp8Q

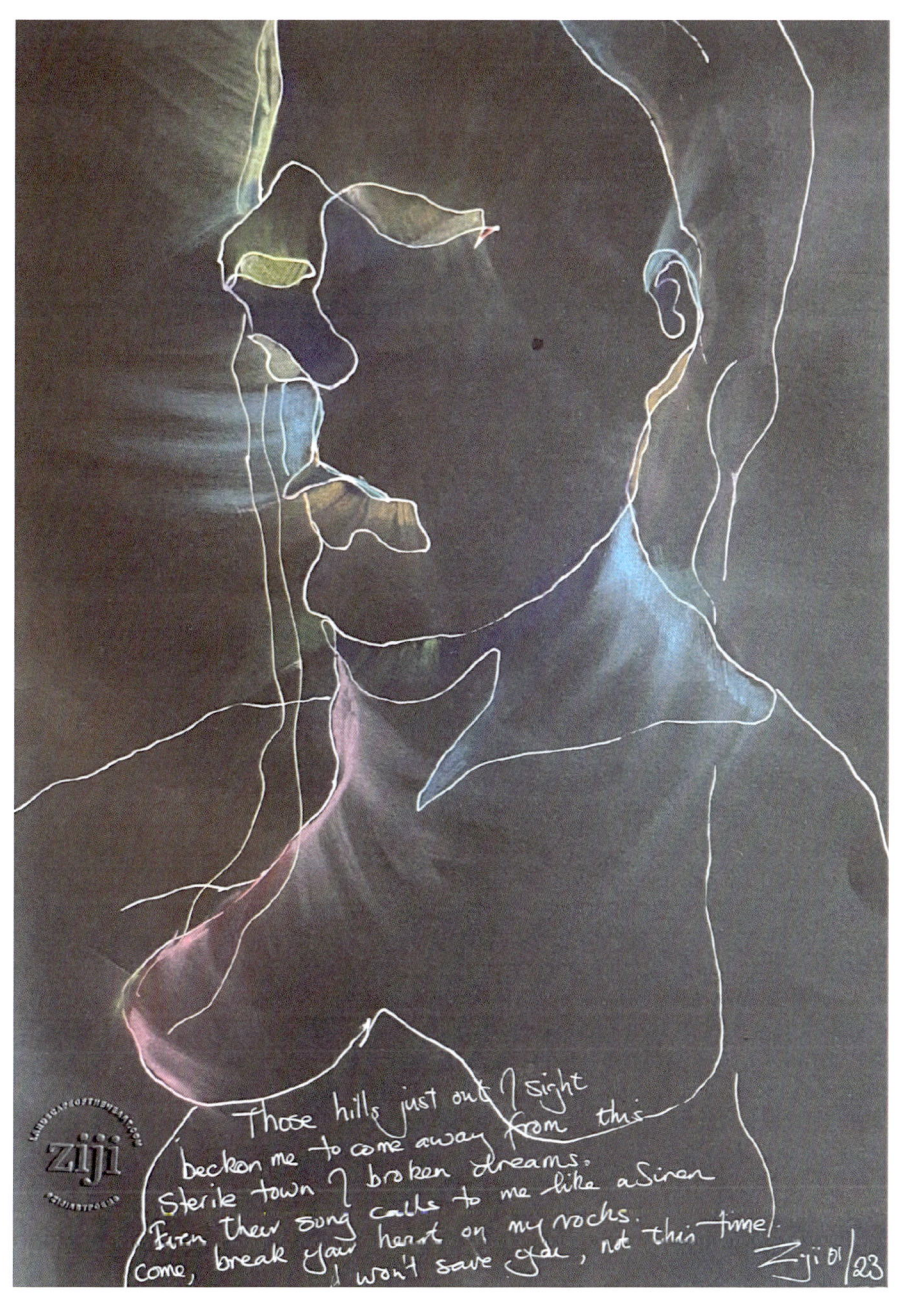

those hills just out of sight
beckon me to come away from this
sterile town of broken dreams.
Even their song calls to me like a siren
come, break your heart on my rocks.
I won't save you, not this time
Ziji 01/23

SELL

After dropping out of vet science, I landed a life changing job with Olims P/L. They are hotel owners, and had a subsidiary called Music Tone, specialising in selling hi-fi music equipment and vinyl records. In my job, I drove from Sunshine Coast Qld. down to Murwillumbah NSW, filling vinyl record orders. There would always be a few spare unaccounted-for records, so the staff would hang around in the storeroom after a delivery from head office, and after a stock count, we'd take the one's not accounted for. Cheap Thrills, Rolling Stones, Janice Joplin. It was fantastic.

My boss was John M, a five-foot five salesman. He taught me how to sell. At the rear of the building behind the beautiful Grundig and Blaupunkt high-fi equipment, we watched customers entering the store. He'd say 'So what do you think, Pete? Where are they from? What school do their kids go to? How many kids have they got? What's their income? What car are they driving? What's their health like?' At first, I had no clue.

But he did. He would guess they most likely lived, for example, in Coorparoo, drove a second-hand car, rented their house, had kids that attended state school and they probably had a budget of $100 - this is 1970. So, he'd instruct me to sell them $100 worth of equipment, because even though they would tell me they have a budget of $200, the truth was they could only afford $100.

And so, enthusiastic salesman-in-training, I would greet the family and they would say that they were looking for high-fi equipment in a $200 price bracket. But John was right, they couldn't afford it. So, I suggested that for a little less, they'd get a better value item. Fascinatingly, throughout the transaction, I discovered that John was accurate in his predictions. They did live in Coorparoo. They did have a second-hand car. They did rent. Their kids did go to state school.

Wow, I thought. I must learn how to do this. And like a sponge, I soaked up Madge's sales methodology.

Customers wandered into the store hoping to buy something they couldn't afford, and I would sell them something cheaper. From the outside, it appeared to be a gesture of goodwill. But really it was about making a sale, and keeping the customer before they went to another store.

I now understand the process was the same as used by Milton Erickson[35] in psychotherapy, and subsequently packaged as NLP by Bandler and Grinder. I learned to read pupil dilation; changes in skin colour and voice tone; breath rate and blood pressure; clues to their internal psychology from movements of the eyes and posture. Even their pheromones might have suggested which customer was for and which was against, how much buy and time pressure each was under. I developed 'unconscious competence'[36] by mirroring John's method.

John and his wife would have me over for dinner. I felt part of their family. Perhaps I could have gone on as a sales rep, selling cars or real estate. Once you have that ability to make a sale, it's a skill applicable anywhere.

I began to consider what I wanted to do with the rest of my life. I was someone I wanted to know and love, and whose life was important. Until then I lived to bury the stranger who abducted me. It was like a beginning of coming out of the dark and loving myself.

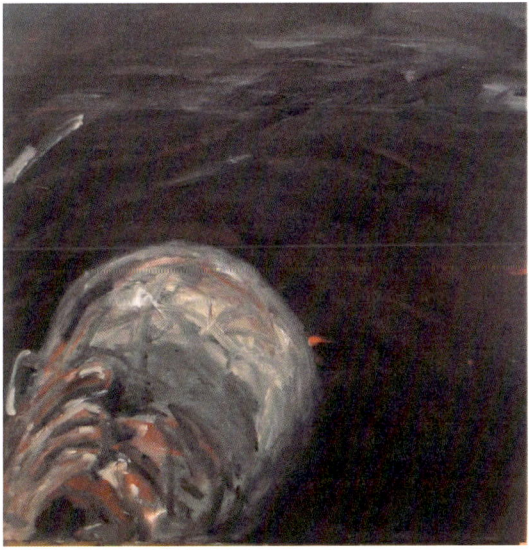

Birth trauma #39

---

[35] https://en.wikipedia.org/wiki/Milton_H._Erickson/

[36] https://en.wikipedia.org/wiki/Four_stages_of_competence/

One of my veterinary friends at the time was Margaret W. Her father was Professor of Psychology. One day, going to meet her at his office, there were a bunch of psychology books displayed for a conference being held at the U of Q. I flicked through them. One caught my attention. It was about the psychology of emotions. I had never heard of psychology, even though that was what John taught me.

I had never heard of *emotions*. I knew I felt bad or angry or sad, however, my emotional vocabulary was limited. And there in the Professor's waiting room was this book. There were words for emotions I had never heard of such as "grief". I had lived with grief my entire life, even before I was born, yet I didn't know there was a word for it.

I rushed home, giving Margaret some excuse for my no-show. I opened the Encyclopaedia Britannica, which in those days was sold door to door, and just drank everything on the subject they had published in the 1965 edition.

In my novel 'The Dream Life of Debris', I sent Paul on a road trip from Brisbane to Adelaide to reunite with his aunt Mary, in a VW Combi whose interior was decorated with pages torn from the Encyclopedia Britannica.

The most powerful thing you can do in therapy is name it and then claim it. It took me a long time to name and claim grief, but at that point in time - I had the word. I was drawn to the language of psychology.

I found a psychology course as far away from dad as I could get, which was Perth.

If you get brutalised enough, you mature very fast. And provided you do not kill yourself; you focus intensely on survival. I had an inner knowing that if I stayed in Brisbane, I would die. Dad drove me insane with his misery, neediness, and suicidality. But he agreed to the idea of me relocating to Sydney to attend the University of New South Wales.

overlapping shields of self hidding ever surest Rowing in the cracks, for you only to read my love

Zajj 7/21

MIND

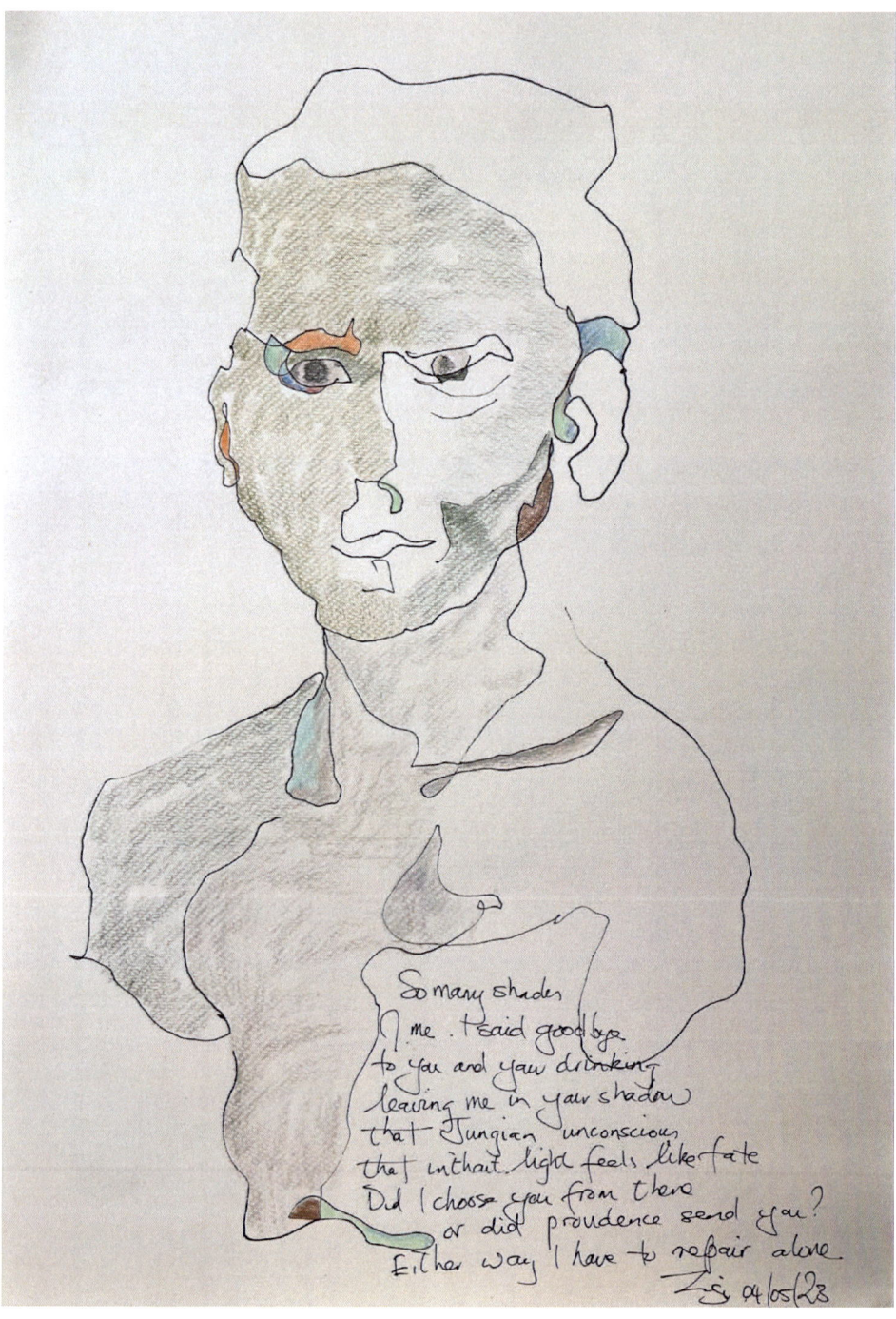

So many shades
Me. I said goodbye
to you and your drinking
leaving me in your shadow
that Jungian unconscious
that without light feels like fate
Did I choose you from there
or did providence send you?
Either way I have to repair alone.
Lis 04/05/23

#40

*So many shades
of me. I said goodbye
to you and your drinking
leaving me in your shadow,
that Jungian unconscious
that without light feels like fate.
Did I choose you from there
or did providence send you?
Either way I have to repair alone.
Ziji 04/05/23*

I arrived at university in the middle of a psychology shitstorm. A massive fight had developed over the previous couple of years between the Hypnotherapists, the Freudians, the Human Potential Movement (HPM) and the Behaviorists.

The Behaviorists were brilliant at getting funding for focused packages that worked: erectile dysfunction and agoraphobia for example. They needed only to flash their credentials around the university, and were granted another senior lecturer, more tutorials and research grants. Consequently, the Behaviorists grew in influence. The others declined.

A group of about twenty of us asked for less theory and more practice. It was in the interests of the Hypnotists, the Freudians, the HPM advocates to give us experience. A psychoanalytic treatment of fear of heights, for example, was then either decades long or interminable.

The Primal Scream of Arthur Janov, originally a one treatment cure for phobias, also became a regular treatment regimen. John Lennon and Yoko Ono were fans of this once sure-fire way of curing the traumatic origins of all neuroses. [37] So, we got in early and had our own encounter groups, primal screams, Car Rogers and unconditional positive regard, and clients to practice on.

We lapped up the anti-psychiatry movement, and later powerfully affected by movies like 'One Flew Over the Cuckoo's Nest' and by RD Laing, whose work became a lens for understanding my origins.[38]

One of our professors ran an experiment where healthy PhD students of his, admitted themselves with fabricated symptoms of paranoia, hallucinations, suicidality, etc to a psychiatric hospital. Once in, they reverted to normal, even describing the research project they were engaged in, the professor supervising and tried to get discharged. One guy couldn't get out without police assistance. His alleged research project was diagnosed by hospital staff as a delusional thought process, thus evidence of their psychosis.

---

[37] https://www.independent.co.uk/news/obituaries/arthur-janov-obituary-primal-scream-psychologist-embraced-by-john-lennon-a7986301.html

[38] https://www.goodreads.com/book/show/32512094-sanity-madness-and-the-family/

I left U of NSW four years later and hit the ground running. I, and some of my fellow graduates, simply knew what to do. There was no doubt that the relationship with our clients depended on rapport. Rapport was the number one thing. It depended on awareness of your own self and what your experience was of that person because that suggested what might be going on inside them. A Behaviorist in the seventies was not primarily interested in rapport. Or their own inner personal experience.

ART AND MIND

One of my lecturers was a professor of Social Psychology interested in the art of schizophrenics and the Haptic art of the blind. Both impacted me. I witnessed how therapy was possible through art and writing. I soaked up Bukowski's visceral, cathartic poems. I was shaping a broad artistic mindfulness.

This was the scaffolding I used to understand the absurdity of life.

Later one of my art heroes Francis Bacon, in my painting below, wrote 'since life is meaningless, we have to make our lives extraordinary.' I too am an optimistic nihilist.

Here's a much later drawn self-portrait, which resonates with how I understood myself in my late teens, early twenties.

*do I age until, sloughing off the masks
the international traveller from the stars
starts to appear. The cosmic dancer
made of dust, clothed in flesh for a short trip
on the green planet,
celebrating timeless travel
in drag
Ziji 02/03/23*

During the four years I soaked up ideas. I simply got it. It was second nature. I'd sit my exams and pass. Maybe I had a brain, I thought and tested it by applying to join Mensa. To get into Mensa, I had to sit their tests and score an IQ between 130 and 150. I did that and went to a meeting. I was there among clever people who just wanted to play bridge, drink expensive wine, and tell you about the whole history of the vineyard it came from. I thought, what am I doing here? These were not my people.

I had a brain, yes. But how did my brain manage to evolve? Because at age eight and later, it's normal development was hijacked by trauma. My body shut down emotionally. I expressed no overt feeling except rage. From an attachment theory[39] point of view I was protesting. My scanning of the environment, and absorption of information was in survival brain mode. Learning brain mode had been dulled by trauma. I experienced the usual post trauma mechanisms of hypervigilance, hyper arousal, dissociation…but I was smart.

I had a 'mental breakdown' in the first year of university. I was on the ceiling looking down at myself. I could not get off the ceiling. A cosmic dancer in deep trouble. The university counsellor I saw might have recommended a psychiatric admission, but he was Rogerian, a Humanist. George Grey saved my life. He could see that what I really needed was quiet and time out.

He organised a stay in the sick bay of a neighbouring college for nearly a week (allegedly with glandular fever). Eventually, I came back down from the ceiling. I did more counselling, more therapy and over time returned to normal. But I medicated with sex, alcohol, cigarettes.

My girlfriend, who would eventually be my first wife and mother of three of my kids, was a fantastic woman. Her family were Holocaust survivors. As a child, she caught the bus to school, and her mother warned her "never tell anybody on the bus who you are, because the Nazis are out to get you".

Our relationship was unconsciously driven by the damages of our childhoods, the intergenerational trauma of our parents and the miracles of survival and healing. Ours was a crazy celebration of life that brought three wonderful kids into the world.

---

[39] https://www.ncbi.nlm.nih.gov/pmc/articles/PMC6920243/

*These tales we tell ourselves are designed in the back of our minds
we slip in and out of the dream of who we might be, staying with the story.
I told you at the beginning, that we were forever.
I can feel the dream
just as I fall asleep and then wake to who I must be.
Ziji 20/05/23*

Threesome #41

We hold these ghosts of relationships past
haunting us with fantasy reliving
and every new one like an archeology dig
excavating beneath the rock and clay
to find the source of ourselves
in the unconscious reprise
of the forgotten. Let the sunshine here and
new life green and
lush sprout between us
Ziji 20/05/23

GO

As a practising psychologist, I was successful. As a salesman and a survivor, I understood many of my clients. I understood their core issues from lived experience, and I could sell them a story of healing.

It made me a capable therapist. I used to think of therapy as open-heart surgery. I spoke with a broken heart that resonated with theirs. However, I couldn't show them something at that time, which only later did I come to reveal - healing of heart and soul.

Truly I have felt blessed in this journey of recovery by the kindness of strangers and the abiding love of friends and family.

I joined a twelve-step sex/love addicts anonymous group of gifted, street-smart people. We all understood each other's stories, and through that support, for better and for worse, eventually two of our marriages broke up.

*Taking these small steps
we come to know those tears
of pleasure, of laughter and rage,
housed in the same body
sometimes as friends of the awakening
others of hiding separating
from what joins us as one
to the One
Ziji 01/23*

Made
whole
in broken
Parts

MARY

Resting there in you, such peace
held in the light and the darkness
I can flower, blossom and die
in the season of us
can this go on forever or will love be
swept away in the next flood or fire?
as long as it's with you we will be
my love, my life
Ziji 9/22

I met Mary five years before my marriage ended. We were friends, in the same yoga group and had many common interests. I was running a Lifeline training group that she attended. She was a few years out of a nine-year stint in a yoga ashram that later became the subject of Royal Commission Case 21 - another sex abusing guru.

Over the time before we got together, I saw her at yoga gatherings. She knew nothing of my growing feelings for her. From her perspective, I was a happily married man.

Underneath there was an incipient nervous breakdown. I didn't end on the ceiling, depersonalised and derealised as I had in first year university. I was on the verge, unaware, of a major episode of decompensation within a PTSD storm. It preceded, coincided with and followed the breakdown of my first marriage.

I first heard the word decompensation at a Harville Hendrix workshop. I was chatting with Harville when he told me he had to take a call from home where a colleague was decompensating. At the time I had no idea what that meant.

Now I understand that it was the trauma memories I had compensated for with alcohol, romance and sex addiction, that were threatening to break through in *sensory, perceptual, emotional,* and *cognitive changes.* [40]

Had I known then what I know now so much of the hurt I inflicted on all my loved ones and on myself, and the toxic shame I have beaten myself up with, could have been avoided or at least better managed. Ah the joys of hindsight!

I blame the government - the generations of ignorance perpetrated in our education systems, where the 3 R's do not include Relationship (except in a mathematical sense) - the primary navigation system of our lives, and the fundamental operating system of our brain, its evolution and its development.[41]

---

[40] https://www.carenity.us/condition-information/magazine/news/what-is-mental-decompensation-1218

[41] https://www.ncbi.nlm.nih.gov/pmc/articles/PMC6920243/

Mary #42

*So perfect this
moment in time
when we breathe
together. Your warmth
fills my lungs with
joy and hope.
The darkness
fades like a
bright moonlit night
all silver and,
in every cell
small voices begin
to sing us
Ziji 9/22*

Love #43

*what are these feelings,
this stirring in the heart
so new to me.
We just met and I sense
my whole world is turning
upside and over down.
Can a turtle turn into a swan
a worm become a butterfly
and yet this is happening in me.
We just met and my world is
transforming around me
without intention but in deep
design of life's plan.
Just let it flow in me and all will be well*
Ziji '21

Aix en Provence #44

*Taken in small steps
even the insurmountable
becomes possible
I meet you on the descent
covered in pine leaves
scent of provence
shall we go down to aix
for a coffee and love?
Ziji 11/05/23*

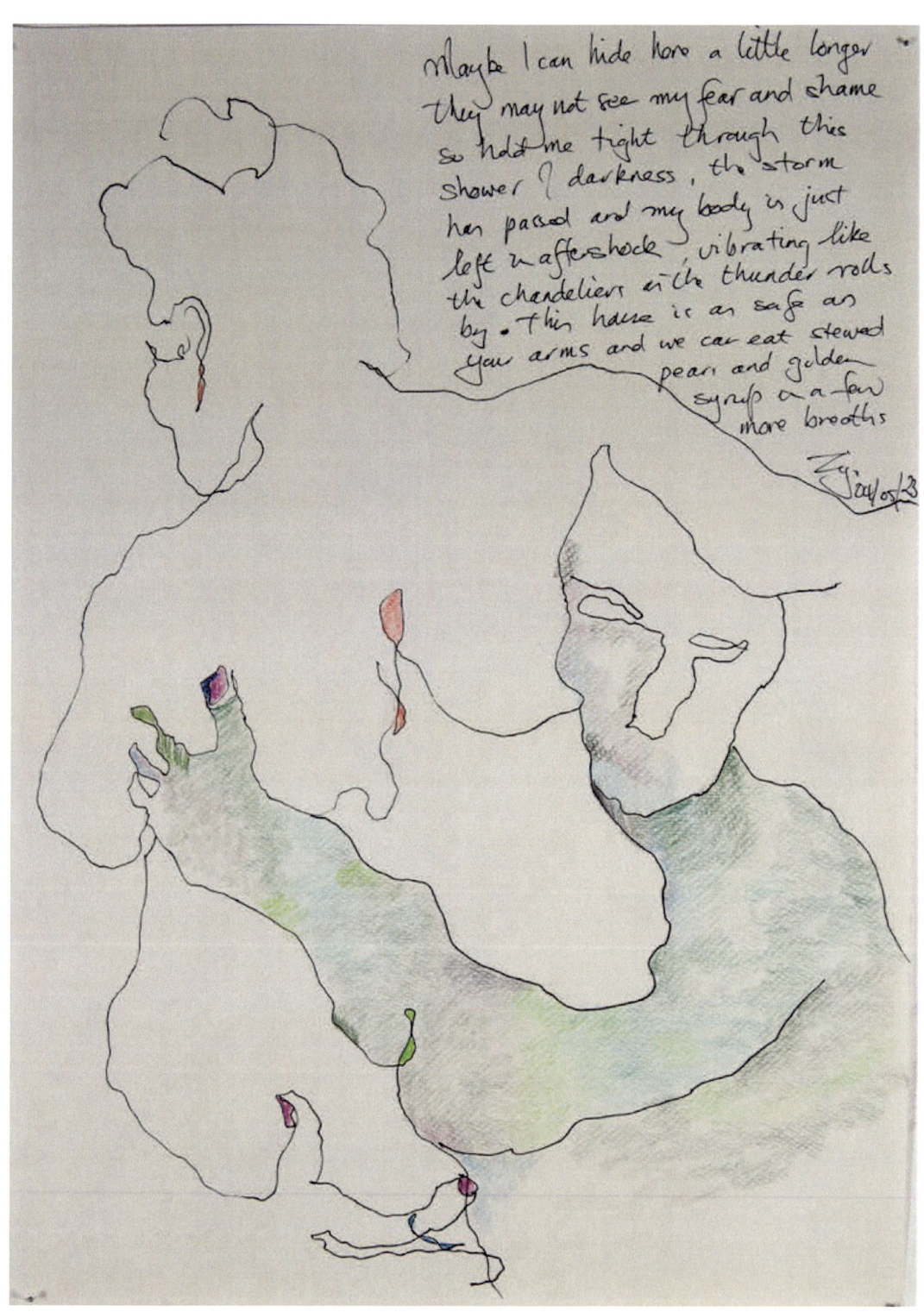

Safe harbour 1. #45

*Maybe I can hide here a little longer
they may not see my fear and shame
so hold me tight through this
shower of darkness, the storm
has passed and my body is just
left in aftershock, vibrating like
the chandeliers as the thunder rolls by.
This house is as safe as
your arms and we can eat stewed
pears and golden
syrup in a few
more breaths
Ziji 04/05/23*

When I eventually left my marriage, I moved into the apartment above the shops where Mary was living. She had an established yoga practice and emanated a deep calm. It was the first time in my life that I came to experience contentment.

I was attending art school through the beginning of that relationship and had begun writing again. We were both fans of Arnie and Amy Mindell's Process Work and spent our early years as a couple in the workshops that two of their colleagues ran in Byron Bay.

Safe harbour 2.

*Where is this wind that carries
the space between us, that lifts us
out of our self-obsession.
Where is the pause in its power
and we hold our breath and look
really see into each other and
know it's the flow that
brings jasmine and frangipani
carries mesalla ginger & lime
into our nostrils, breathing
in again. ah, it is us
in the wind both cause & effect
Ziji 11/21*

Safe harbour 3.

Laid back in the arms
of life
I hold you safe and secure
You can rest in me in this
land sea of wellness
crested with each breath
tide, tidal food and water
hold you as you melt into me
Ziji '21

*I hold myself
in the wonder of
remembering you
my sweet friend.
The hours we lay in
one anothers arms,
Chest to breat
loins to legs
Oh how I miss that
fragrance of love making
the rhythm of our sex
I hold myself remembering
Us, soothing me in this
moment when I am alone.
Ziji '21*

My Dear Old Dad

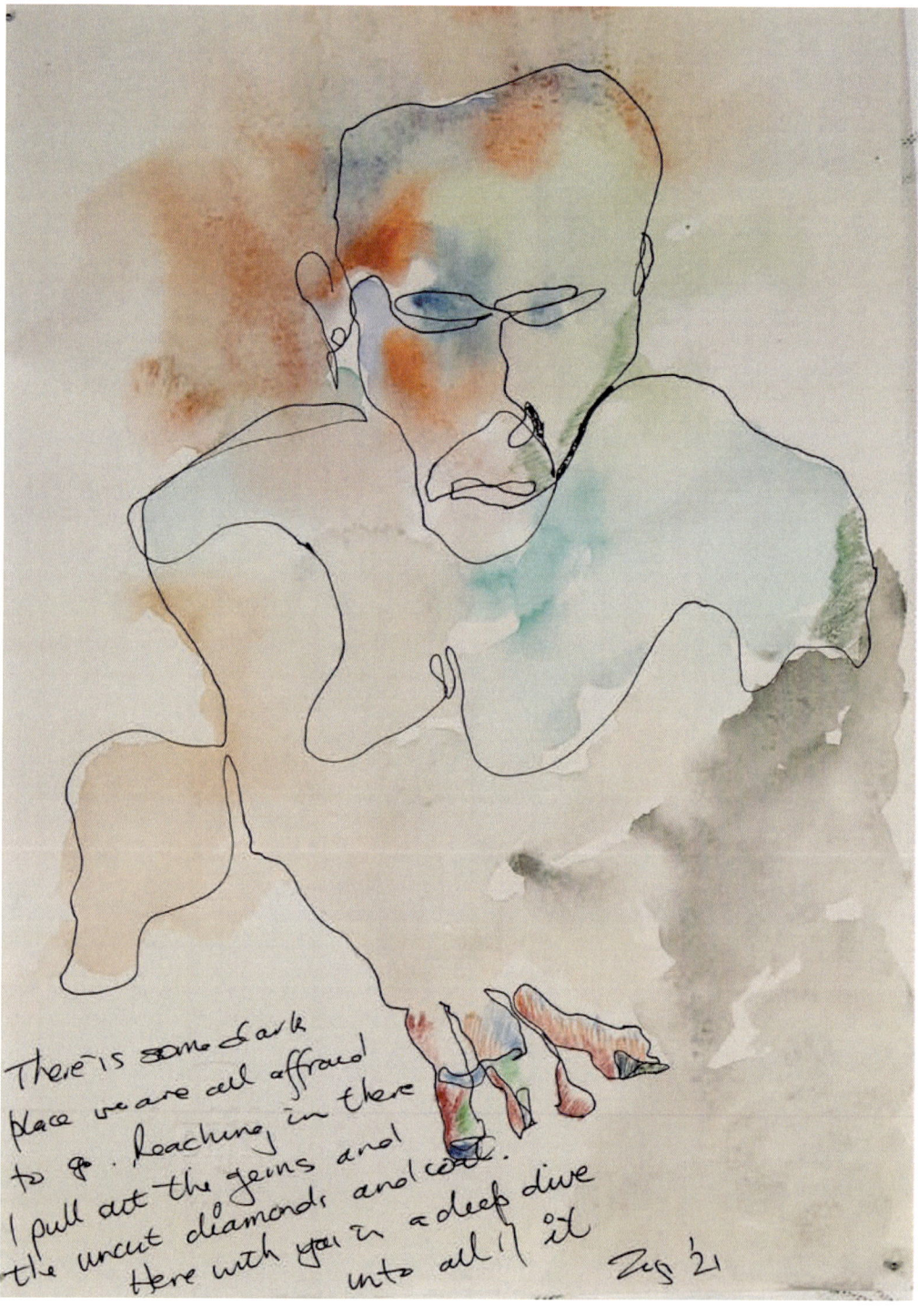

> *There is some dark place we are all afraid to go. Reaching in there I pull out the gems and the uncut diamonds and coal. Here with you is a deep dive into all of it*
> *Ziji '21*

I haven't mentioned many good things about my dad, my first cousin once removed! For all his troubles, war trauma and anxiety, so like my own, he had my back most of the time. He loved me as best he could. A wonderful cook, fascinated by history, religion and psychology. He was an architect by profession, chosen for him by his parents who were Estate Agents in the UK.

But his passion was the share market. I learnt how to and how not to trade. I later made the same mistakes that I criticised him for. He loved the bush; he was an early bush regenerator. Wherever we lived, we owned a bush block. We would tidy up the bush; lay trees he fell on the contours; fill in gutters created by erosion with boulders, and plant trees appropriate to the environment.

He was a hunting, shooting, fishing kind of dad. He taught me how to make trout fishing flies, and then we would go fishing in the snowy mountains for rainbow trout. We'd go rabbiting with ferrets and guns. Camp on the beach in a beaten-up old Land Rover and a trailer with a canvas roof. Some of my happiest memories of him.

Underneath all the damage and the wounding, dad was a child of nature. Just a boy. And I didn't really meet that child until eighteen months before he died, when he started to drop everything.

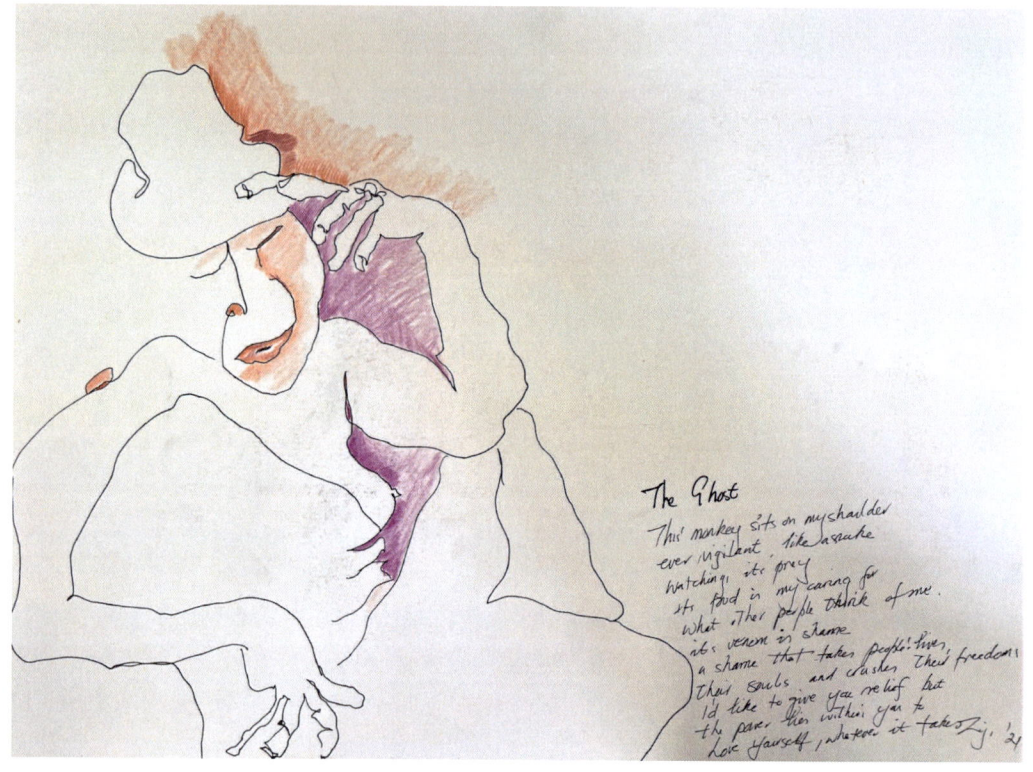

The Ghost

*This monkey sits on my shoulder
ever vigilant, like a snake
watching its prey
its food is my caring for
what other people think of me.
Its venom is shame
a shame that takes people's lives
their souls and crushes their freedoms.
I'd like to give you relief but
the power lies with you to
love yourself, whatever it takes.
Ziji '21*

In yogic theory there are three energetic knots or granthis that lock us into the body.[42] We can learn to soften these with breath practices and bandhas. It is usually difficult to leave the body without our death. Out of body experiences[43] are one way we might leave the body, as are near death experiences or reversible clinical death.[44]

As my dad was dying, all those knots started to relax. And when that happened…. that boy appeared. A beautiful, sweet, innocent, lovely kid. That was the first time I met my father. It was another gift. Dad died at home. I wanted to kill him the second he breathed his last. Seriously!

Suddenly I had no-one else to blame. I remembered a client of mine who every year would watch the State of Origin final with her husband. It was a bonding ritual over many decades. When he died in the middle of the final, she told me she burst into anger that he had stolen their enjoyment of the match. How dare he die. I had a similar and different experience when my dad passed. He took away my excuse.

There's a boy inside me; undamaged, unheard, probably pre-birth who has been blasting his way out. I now want to give this kid the maximum amount of freedom from my adult performative, well-adapted, brilliant self. I want this kid to tell me what's going on in the back of mind.

That's why I call it excavating the unconscious. I want him and her to show up. I don't want to be told. I don't want to analyse in the moment. I let the pen and the poem lead me. I want to get out of the way of this process and just be.

---

[42]'A simpler way to understand granthis is to think of each knot as a silo of our complexes, unconscious fears, and mental/emotional/physical conditioning. They create impulses up on which we act, box us in our identity, and bind us to our limitations.'
https://www.prana-sutra.com/post/the-three-granthis-yoga-brahma-vishnu-rudra/

[43] https://en.wikipedia.org/wiki/Out-of-body_experience

[44] https://en.wikipedia.org/wiki/Near-death_experience

Landscape #46

> We can place this moment in memory
> by the scent of sandalwood and jasmine
> that comes to us in the sweetness
> of our love nest in the trees.
> These humans look and no longer smell
> the strangeness that is coming
> to their world
> *Ziji 11/23*

TRAUMA

There was a man who ran a trucking company in Australia. He was a World War II pilot who carried damaging experiences from the war. He suffered with classic post-traumatic stress, tormented by the whole panoply of PTSD symptoms. He'd heard about a woman named Francine Shapiro who was having success working with treatment resistant war veterans suffering PTSD.

Francine was a Buddhist. She discovered Eye Movement Desensitization and Reprocessing, known as EMD*R. She stumbled on it one day while walking in a park. She had breast cancer and wondered about the anxiety she was feeling around losing part of her breast. She started to flick her eyes back and forth. The distress she felt started to subside. Being a Behaviorist, she was curious about the mechanism of that effect. She then thought of another upsetting moment and continued to move her eyes back and forth. Again, the anxiety subsided.

She called her friends who were social workers, physicists, musicians and the like, and asked them to do an experiment for her. They were to think of a recent upset whilst flicking their eyes back and forth. They all did it and all felt the same positive effect.

Francine convinced the US Department of Veteran Affairs to fund a treatment program for the most traumatised Vietnam vets. In the first trial of EMD*R, I think 60% of the vets who completed that program and who had been unable to live without alcohol, drugs, unemployment benefits, got back into life over the course of the following two years.

Our truck driver here in Australia heard about it. He went over to the USA and after experiencing EMD*R with Francine, had his first good sleep ever. No longer triggered. He came back to Australia and spoke to the Psychology Society about what he had found. He offered to pay for Shapiro and her senior trainers to come to Australia. He introduced Psychology Australia to EMD*R for free.

I thought this was amazing. And by the way... what is trauma? I was then in my late thirties and had worked with incest survivors, undercover police officers, rape victims, even staff of a bank hold up, but I had not once considered my own trauma.

Not for a minute had I believed that I had any kind of trauma at all. I then found I had two words to claim my injury – traumatic grief. I only claimed 'complex' years later when I came to understand C-PTSD described my history and my experience of multiple relationship trauma.45

iPhone photo #47

---

45 https://www.psychologytoday.com/us/blog/traumatization-and-its-aftermath/202405/7-myths-about-trauma

*Tasted and then denied
we play an exquisite teasing
torture on our climb to the roof
of the world. Stations on the way
guided by our body's sherpa,
we reach more deeply into the dark
unknown and discover another cave to
open in the light of love*

Ziji 20/02/23

I started receiving EMD*R as a client, and then as a practitioner. The effect was amazing.

It revolutionised my understanding of the brain just by a simple alternating movement: sound, following a hand, watching lights or a windscreen wiper. Bilateral stimulation reminds the brain of its innate healing ability, and the brain begins to rebuild itself.

Suddenly it made perfect sense of what I had done with my trauma. In traumatic shock, the brain breaks up the experience into every sensory category – it locks taste over there, sound in another place, movement there, kinaesthetic there. It fragments the whole experience so the organism can survive. Brilliant compartmentalising so the organism can go on. And when Francine discovered bilateral stimulation, it brought these things from all the corners of the brain and behind the mind back into a moment where they could be processed. And then the brain picks it up and declares that it remembers how to mend.

I started using EMD*R and I got better results than from any other method. I watched the windscreen wipers; sat in the trauma memories I didn't know I had and worked with them. I began to understand how deeply traumatised I had been. I had never thought that was me. And like all deep brain traumas, I had developed coping mechanisms: performative and numbing. I still live with hyper-vigilance, hyper-arousal, and dissociation but I catch it quicker, and self soothe most of the time, without harming myself or my loved ones.

All these coping mechanisms saved my life in a way. I approached my own trauma with care and respect for the way it had protected me throughout my life. The way my brain dealt with it all. And that led me to bodywork. I hadn't found talking therapy at all useful. But massage, breath awareness, rebirthing and sexological bodywork have been helpful and taught me to trust my body.

Bessel Van Der Kolk, in his aptly titled book "The Body Keeps the Score" he suggests that if you don't go and work with a trauma therapist, at least do sculpting or some kind of art because from his observation it has therapeutic value. It somehow initiates bilateral stimulation.

In my work I do right brain drawing and left brain writing. When the paintings are truthful, I believe I am successfully manifesting bilateral stimulation. When I am manipulating it, then it's left brain. And I can see it in premeditated art/poems.

I think trauma therapy is happening with each piece. I dig out stuff from the back of my brain and when I put it down, I almost catch myself wanting to stop the process. I want to refrain from saying something shameful or drawing something exposing. But I just pull back, and let it come. It's not always easy but when you can get out of the way of your thoughts, it is a triumph.

The trick is to let it happen. Don't think about it. If I catch myself thinking, that might be a form of dissociation, so I slow down and move my awareness into my body. Breathe into the fear and let go.

#48

Watching me watching you
in ecstasy, I am made whole
our bodies repaired and grown anew
we are survivors/thrivers of this journey
we brothers and sisters of amethyst
in cancer cells – get to live a second and third life
so many blessings, thankyou life.
Ziji 03/24

*Shadows make
me whole-hidden.
grow me toward
twilight and I
will glow in
shadow and you
will then see me
where i hide the
best parts of me
my sweet love
Ziji 2021*

COUPLE THERAPY #49

Once a week for a couple of months in 2023, I saw a couple at nine o'clock for ninety minutes. Afterwards, Saskia would turn up. We would breathe together, and then remove our clothes. I would draw her and sometimes suggest a theme. Sometimes I would move my art table around her, other times she would move to a new pose. It was the process of getting out of the way and letting whatever wants to come out, to come through the resistance to knowing and feeling.

And, then after the art session, the next client would arrive and I was suddenly speaking *poetry* to them.

There was one occasion when I started speaking to a couple about the *soul* of marriage and how the spirit that brought them together was like a star, and it somehow linked them so that they came together to do this amazing work together in making a family.

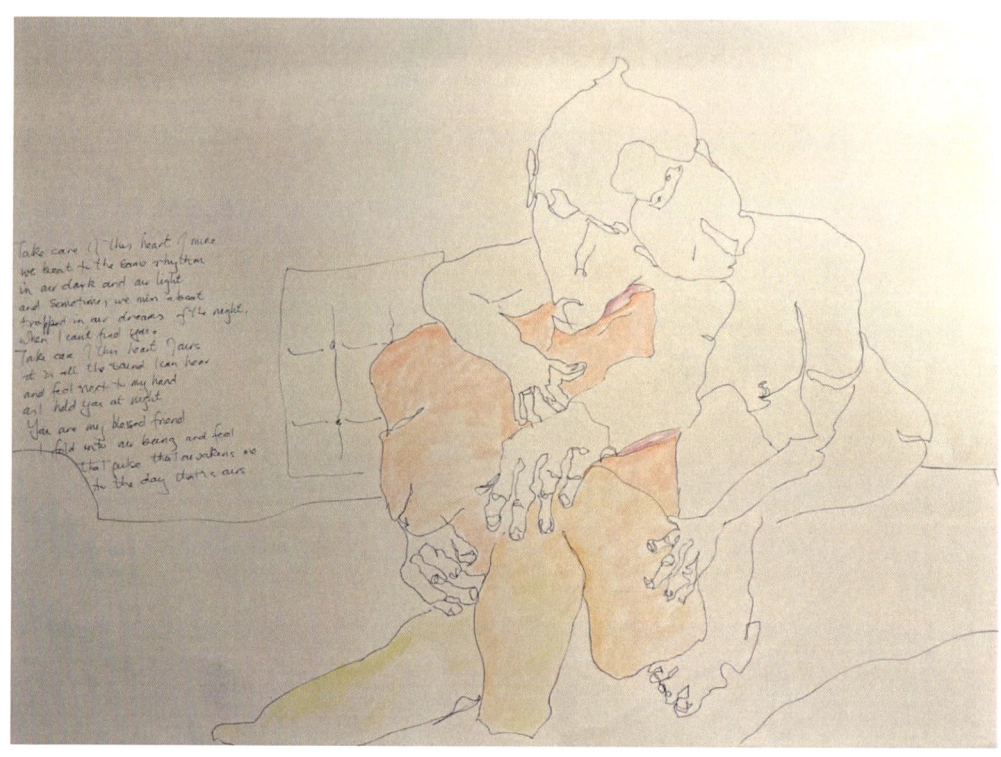

Delicious #50

> *Take care of this heart of mine*
> *we beat to the same rhythm*
> *in our dark and our light*
> *and sometimes we miss a beat*
> *trapped in our dreams of the night,*
> *when I can't find you.*
> *Take care of this heart of ours*
> *it is all the sound I can hear*
> *and feel next to my hand*
> *as I hold you at night.*
> *You are my blessed friend*
> *I fold into our being and feel*
> *that pulse that awakens me*
> *to the day that is ours.*
> *Ziji 07/22*

I said they had been given a gift that will help them evolve in their hearts and souls. They wanted to end the marriage with two young kids in tow because she couldn't stand his narcissism, and he couldn't stand her criticism. Well, I get it - he was narcissistic and abandoned her! And she criticised and shamed him!

But – there was another reference point, I said, that was just as important. And it's this: you have a duty to work with each other the best way you can (it may be together as a couple or not) to create the kind of spiritual nourishment that your children need. Otherwise, someone like me will be seeing them when they reproduce your marriage in 25 years' time.

They were both in tears.

When the next client came along, I couldn't find the same ability to speak soulfully.

My art poetry practice sometimes brings me into a moment of truth. Somebody gets the benefit of it, and then it's back to everyday consciousness. It's so much to do with what the couple bring with them.

For example, the client couple in the next poem (not the models) tells the story of what they brought with them, the sadness of the loss of a sweet young love and the anger and blame that maintained their angry protest, preventing connection and growth. 'Have you some love left for me', one said.

I didn't feel at all creative with them. My job there was as a fire fighter – manage the fuel, put out the fires, cool the pattern until stability returns. But they left me with the next poem 'apple seed and wine' that came out a couple of days later.

The poem 'no straight message from whole body' on page 135, was from another client couple (not the models), who were caught in a death spiral like a murderous addiction to pain.

*apple seed and wine glasses filled
I treasure you and hold every part of
you as if you were that rose in
your garden, sweetly scented
drifting in my nerves
overwhelming my defences
have you some love for me
a night tobacco that wanders
in your dreams of bliss?
Ziji 9/19*

Landscape of the heart

>no straight message from whole
>body, legs and arms speak
>different languages
>come go stay leave grab
>be with me and my
>double tripe signals
>be close to you as I push
>you away
>hold me, throw me
>away
>bite me eat me live
>and re-surrect another day.
>Blind to your games
>Turning away
>Yet always held in your Sway.
>Ziji 9/19

Grieving before I die #51

So many tables on which we can lay our plates and surround the strawberry rose centre with olives peaches and unpasteurised cheese. Follow with affogato and sweet sherry and then we notice our tables' empty and alone. Did we imagine the other laid with us? Did we make it all up eating the fruits of our harvest? Love is like that- a table with our favourite things, senses alive like a movie of all our fantasies and then,
we wake up and are alone.
Oh these memories are so sweet and nourishing a tableau of the dearest moments of my life.
Can I do it just one more time before i die?
Ziji 08/22

Maybe I have a gift that helps people. I don't own it in a proprietorial sense – more so I feel it belongs to life. I've just found a song that sometimes has a universal quality to it. The way some music touches people but not others.

I hope to offer my story to the people I love and my friends and community to help them find a way to discover theirs. I want to show people that they can come through a shitty life and still give. They don't have to sit on the toilet constantly shitting out their miseries. They can get out there and give. For me, it's a casting off. All of life is a casting off.

And it all begins in the fallopian tube. In the beginning, we're travelling in a little ball of consciousness down the fallopian tube. I believe in that week's journey to the womb, we're in cosmic consciousness, an experience is never forgotten and yet is often disavowed. We come out into the womb, implant, and begin to grow our own placenta.

Connected at last to human flesh, we are suddenly dependent and faced with all the problems of attachment, where I believe the human condition begins. Attachment: is it secure? Is it safe? Is she mine? Do I matter? Has she got my back? All the issues of attachment. But before all that shit, we were floating in the cosmos, coming down the fallopian tube bathed in cosmic awareness. I believe we retain that knowledge at a cellular level all our lives. And death or near death bring it back to us.

We live. Hopefully a full and meaningful life. And then we die.

Some people are aware enough to die consciously.

I wish that for myself and for all of us.[46]

---

[40] "This life I have made is too small. It doesn't allow enough in: enough ideas, enough beliefs, enough encounters with the exuberant magic of existence. I have been so keen to deny it, to veer deliberately towards the rational, to cling solely to the experiences that are directly observable by others. Only now, when everything is taken away, can I see what a folly this is. I don't want that life anymore. I want what [the] ancients had: to be able to talk to god. Not in a personal sense, to a distant figure who is unfathomably wise, but to have a direct encounter with the flow of things, a communication without words.

"I want to let something break in me, some dam that has been shoring up this shamefully atavistic sense of the magic behind all things, the tingle of intelligence that was always waiting for me when I came to tap in. I want to feel that raw, elemental awe that my ancestors felt, rather than my tame, explained modern version. I want to prise open the confines of my skull and let in a flood of light and air and mystery... I want to retain what the quiet reveals, the small voices whose whispers can be heard only when everything falls silent." Katherine May https://www.themarginalian.org/2023/03/04/katherine-may-enchantment/

Epitaph #52

*We are a planet in our
many facets.
Our closest friends are surprised
when finally our life is celebrated.
A multitude of selves, sometimes
our best parts, hidden, not from shame
but deep longing for privacy. Stolen
from us as children.
sometimes this is darkness felt in the guts
but mostly it is a shining radiant beauty
hidden until death is near
and the body
reveals its secrets.
Opening at last to light and life.
May you shine now & evermore my love
Ziji 16/02/23*

AFTER

Every love story has three phases that form a circle: harmony, disharmony, and repair. These art poems touch on each, sometimes from a moment and others over a lifetime. Disillusionment brings the darkest of omens, demanding the widest reach into our shared humanity.

Bodies that merge and intertwine with another often show up in my art. These are porous bodies, where one flows into the other. Skin makes this physically impossible, but energetically it happens all the time. I experience us all as indivisible, boundless. We are interwoven with one another.

We know this with a mother and her newborn. We feel this with lovers.

*Make me one and
whole again in
your loving arms.
I have lost my way
and now am found
in your enveloping warmth*

Ziji '21

Intergenerational trauma and healing suggest it's not limited by time.

I spent much of my childhood trying to decipher the unspoken. My caretakers resided in a space where vital experience was unspoken. I had to work things out by myself, gravitating toward the unspoken. I assess many situations, working out how I fit into another's story. Perhaps it is a survival instinct. I ask myself, who is holding the ace in the pack and what cards can I play? How do I make myself useful to them so they will keep me?

Having to relate to my birth mother post-mortem was a gift of my survival. Even though she died giving birth to me, I *knew* that she loved me. I *knew* she had to have me, even though it cost her life. After already losing my two siblings before I was born, she must have known it was risky business. Being conceived only months after the death of my brother and sister, I believe the desire and love for me was monumental.

I experienced a continuation of that intra uterine bond. It wasn't broken by her death. I received that gift at a huge cost.

I was in the hospital where I was born and she died, for two weeks or so. My maternal grandparents and my mother's sister didn't want to take me in. My British Navy maternal grandfather had decided that I killed my mother. His family would have nothing to do with me.

Complicated grief denied, violates the living.

It fell to my mother's friends to foster me for six months whilst hoping my family would get themselves together. They didn't. My foster parents could not have known of my grandparents' crazy way of dealing with complicated grief by denying my existence.

I have imagined myself at two weeks old in a hospital seeking out someone to attach myself to, scanning the energy and body language of strangers. And not finding that resonance, I retreated to some sort of internal relationship with the sensory afterimage of my deceased birth mother.

*Reflections in
our immortality
plan, where I
begin and you
conclude…
love is the
way, only
one
Ziji '21*

I began my life with a deep transpersonal knowledge. Perhaps an angel had shown my life to me before blowing out the candle of prenatal awareness. If I had known what lay ahead of me, I sometimes have thought I would have chosen to die, rather than my mother.

I don't use art consciously as therapy because if I did, it would alter the natural flow. When I create, I'm in a river and I just need to be in the river. If the river has a motive or function, then I have already imposed a layer of analysis on it which will inhibit the flow.

I just get into the river and whatever comes out, I must accept and witness. I give myself maximum of 40 minutes to do it. Some take 20.

My feeling is to put down art without censorship, manipulation, or therapeutic processing. I never know where it's going, and I don't even care. I just know I have got to get into the river and let it out.

I too am porous. For the most part, I cannot retract my antenna. I walk into a room and immediately recognise the energy. And other people respond to this. Some I have never met before, tell me their life story, or share confessions, grievances, and disappointments with me at the post office, the bank, in the street. At times it's too much.

Some of what I absorb from others, whether they are strangers, clients or those close to me, is reflected in my art. My art practice is the place where I experience freedom from being switched on, where I'm not constantly engaging in reading the room.

Many of my poems are about grief, reunion, repair, and reconnection. Some are about a longing for re-creation, and about the human condition. Others are about lust and love.

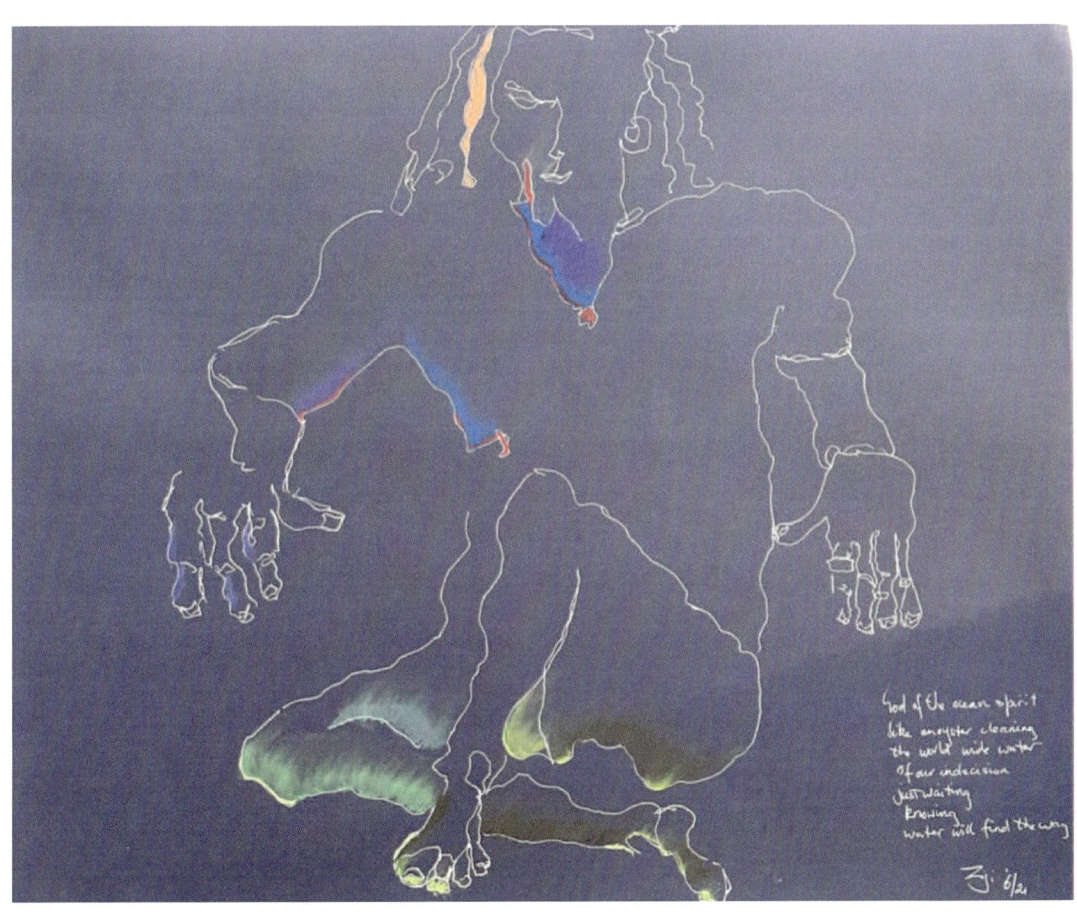

God of the ocean spirit
like an oyster cleaning
the world-wide water
of our indecision
just waiting
knowing
water will find the way
Ziji '6/21

Light within #53

landscape of the heart cxvii

*this boundary between us is
porous, open to all our feelings
through the side, left field entry.
you take me by surprise my darling
suddenly you are inside me, your
spirit flowing like syrup, sweet
delicious in every cell. and
then
you depart and the essence of you
lingers in my heart and soul.
we can never part as long as these
boundaries are freely open to each other.
Ziji 2/22*

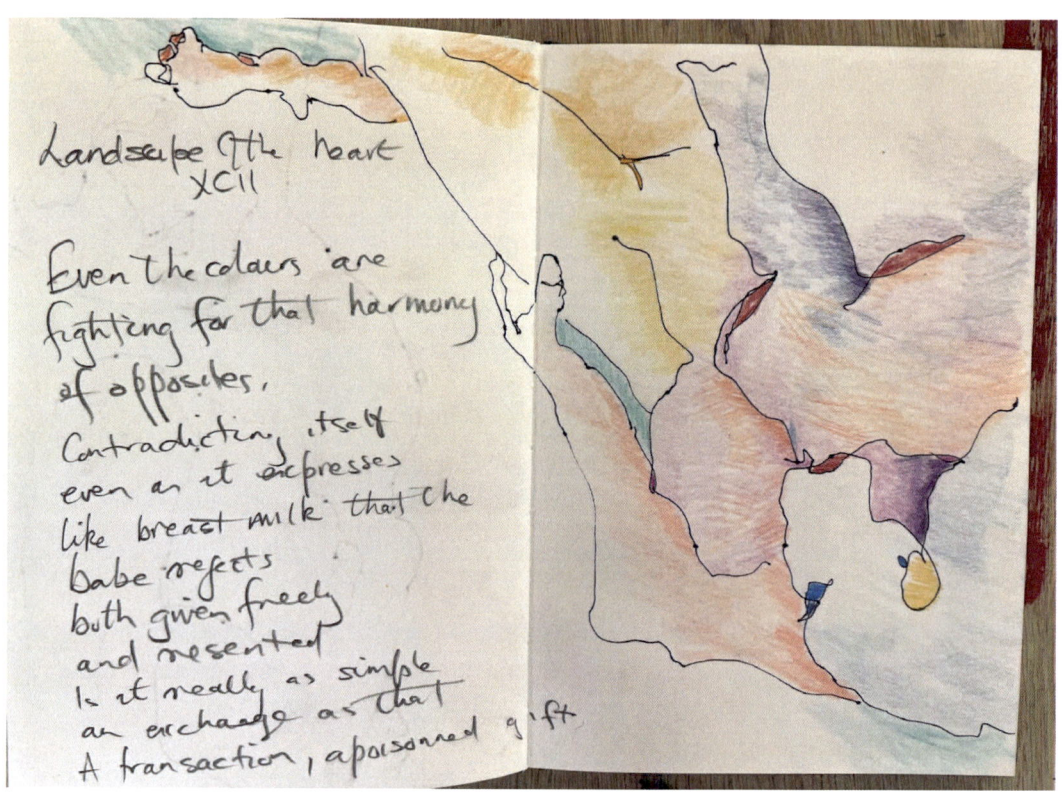

Feb 2022 #54

landscape of the heart xcii

*even the colours are
fighting for that harmony
of opposites.
Contradicting itself
even as it express
like breast milk that the
babe rejects
both given freely
and resented.
Is it really as simple
an exchange as that?
A transaction, a poisoned gift*

Every painting here is autobiographical, but some are more obvious than others.

Birth #2

This is an image of the smash and grab emergency caesarean section from which I was born, my mother haemorrhaging and I in respiratory distress. The patron Saint of such birth and death arrivals is Raymond Nonatus. [47]

To quote AI's response footnoted here [48] *a child who has experienced significant early trauma may be more likely to have a heightened response to later traumatic events, potentially leading to an increased risk of psychological conditions such as PTSD, anxiety, or depression. Each layer of trauma can exacerbate the effects of the others, leading to complex challenges in adulthood. The potential impacts on the adult child can be profound and multifaceted.*

It's incredible to me that I survived and am functioning quite well in my 70's.

---

[47] https://en.wikipedia.org/wiki/Raymond_Nonnatus

[48] https://chat.openai.com/share/63f23a19-622a-463c-96fb-7aca7f06bb01

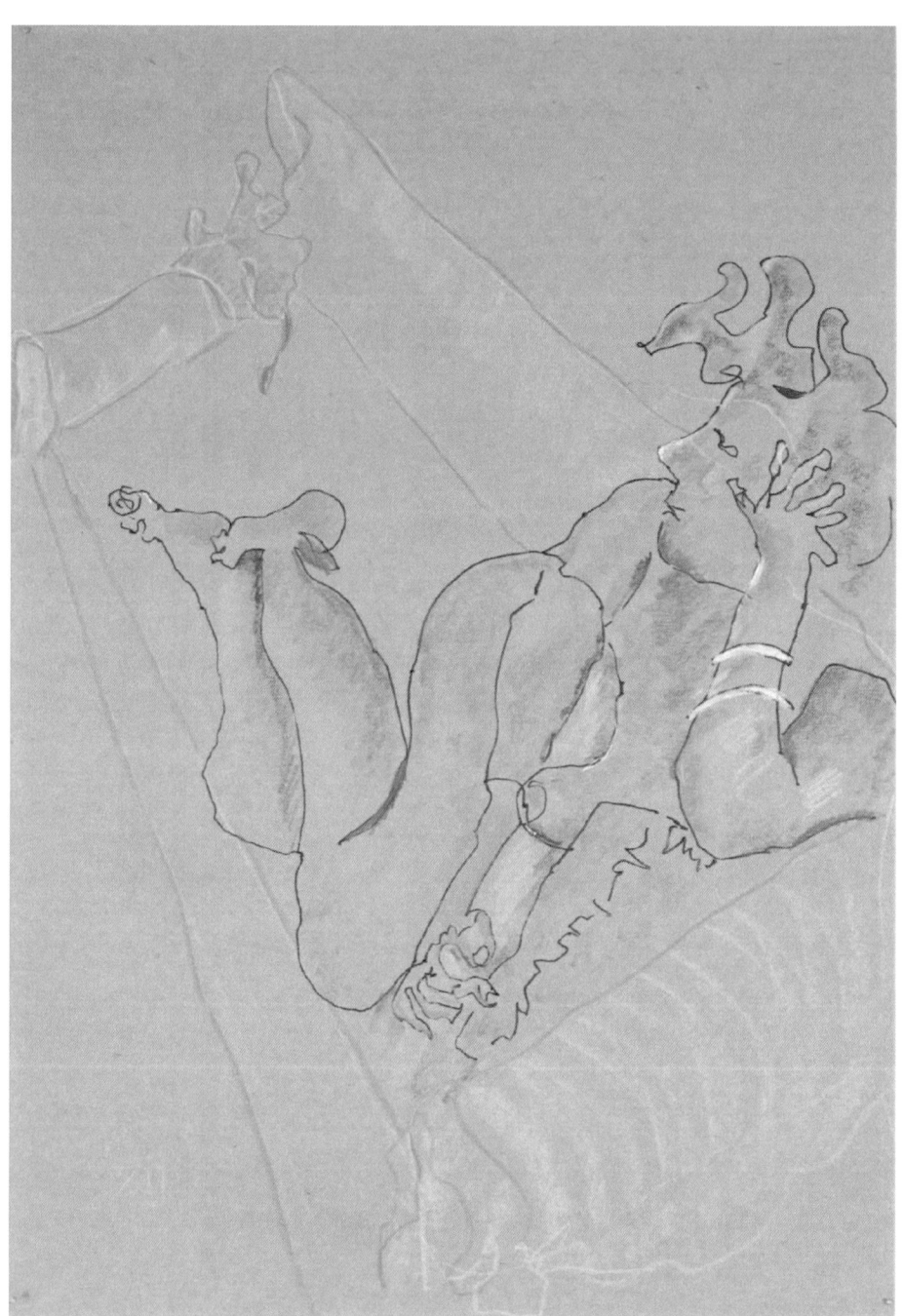

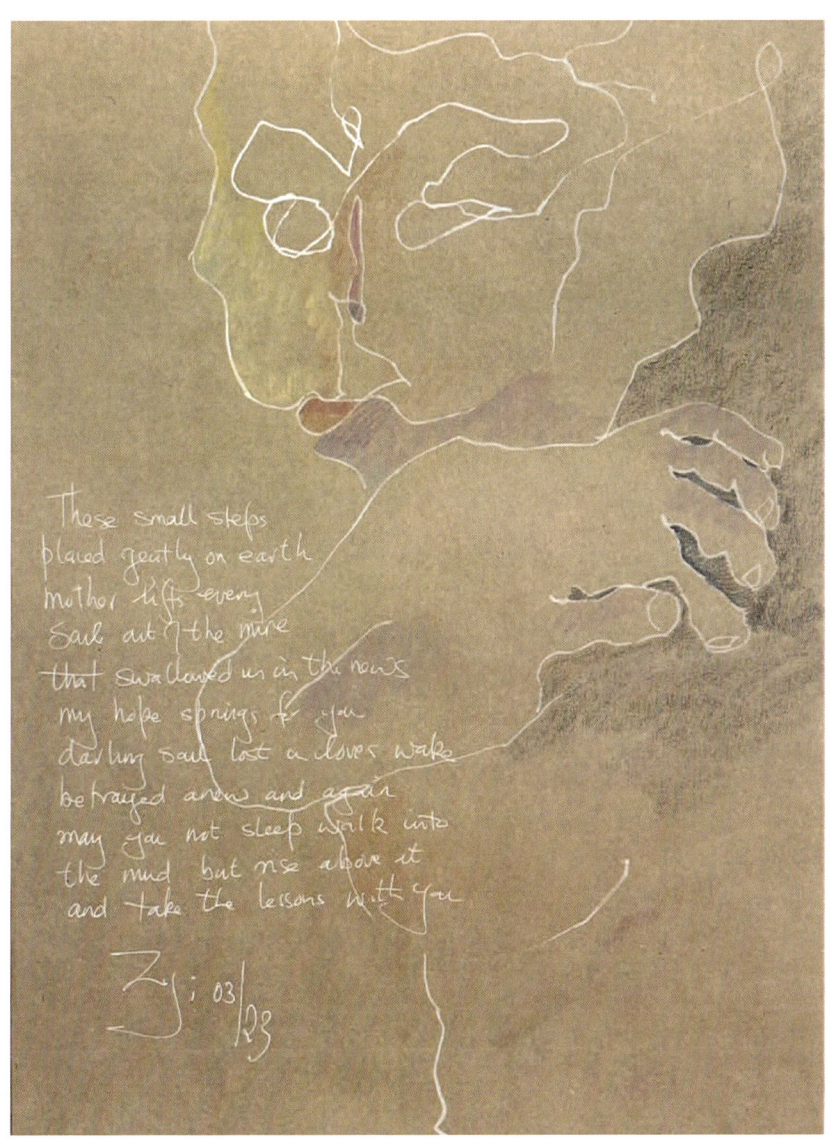

These small steps
placed gently on earth
mother lifts every
soul out of the mire
that swallowed us in the news
my hope springs for you
darling soul lost in lover's wake
betrayed anew and again
may you not sleep walk into
the mud but rise above it
and take the lessons with you
Ziji 03/23

Porous body

The idea of the porous body for me is linked to Sufi mysticism, esoteric physiology, yoga spirituality and Jewish mysticism. So many of us wonder… what is beyond the physical body? At some point, many people have experienced a deep transpersonal knowing. So, what is that transmission about?

A useful analogy of a porous body is the non-abrasive kitchen sponge. The sponge is obviously very porous. If one were piled on top of another you might imagine it as a multi layered sheath or envelope around the body. Imagined that as a rainbow container of energy that each of us travels within, coloured at every level, shimmering with light. It is the subtle vehicle in which we incarnate and embody. We think 'body' is primary. We say we came into this world, not we came out of life. We came 'where the wave of life bursts into individual, sparkling and multicoloured drops that gleam for a moment … a unique action of the total universe.'[49]

At each layer of energy, we are susceptible to different experiences entering our field, until it reaches one of the imagined kitchen sponges denser non-abrasive sections, a boundary of sorts, which is where we have some sort of choice (though to some degree we are still porous through all layers). The question is, do we let it in, or do we ignore it?

When relating to the ones we love and have little resistance to, the denser layer is more open to influence. Sometimes we can feel them from the other side of the world, just as if they are in front of us speaking directly to us. The energy just pours through us and between us, touching our unknowing. Is it the same when we sleep with them?

Most people believe that a person or soul is contained within the confines of the body. And all thought occurs in the brain. But these are not true. I don't end at my skin, and neither do you. My thoughts are embodied. There is a mingling, an association of

---

[49] We do not "come into" this world; we come out of it, as leaves from a tree. As the ocean "waves," the universe "peoples." Every individual is an expression of the whole realm of nature, a unique action of the total universe. This fact is rarely, if ever, experienced by most individuals. Even those who know it to be true in theory do not sense or feel it but continue to be aware of themselves as isolated "egos" inside bags of skin.'
Alan Watts in <u>The Book: On the Taboo Against Knowing Who You Are</u>

energy and information between us, and within us, always. And when a connection is richly developed between two people, they can read one another clearly. This is because we are constantly and unconsciously melding, massaging this cloud of information. Sometimes we tune into it and sometimes we don't. Sometimes it slaps us into an awakening, and sometimes we prefer sleep.

Porous body is transpersonal. It is beyond time and place and is not limited by any geographical distance. So, when that fertilised egg comes floating down the fallopian tube, it's in this limitless space. If you could attribute consciousness to that little zygote, it is beyond touch, beyond sound, beyond sight. Rather it is a core essential sense. It isn't any of the things we think of as limited to our bodies. It's sensory, it's felt and is of an eternal deeper knowing.

Take all you pleasure in me life – I surrender to you you have my back and I give you my all.

Flood and fire #55

This place you take me too
so strange in its wildness
and loss.
This place a new landscape every morning
magnificent and terrifying.
will I sleep in this place tonight
I dream of the house rumbling and shattering
and yet I wake
and you are there, eyes open heart melting
my one true love, in this place
you take me too ...
so strange in your wildness.
this place is ours for eternity
Ziji 5/22

Frightened #56

> There are places in here we hardly
> know, until
> in a brief slice in the fabric of time
> on a lonely road
> one speaks to us, from a time
> long forgotten; we are
> just held in a fragment of memory
> long enough to know our source,
> the fruit of many lives,
> and one speaks to us
> 'it's going to be okay
> you are in a sea of wellness'
> just rest here and breathe
> for a moment of time
>
> Ziji 7/22

There is a mystic Hebrew story that just before the soul incarnates at conception, an angel comes into awareness. It shows the soul, about to travel down the fallopian tube and embody, the entirety of their life by lighting a candle. The candle illuminates the whole of the life they are about to live, the lives they have previously lived and how it is all one continuous journey.

And then, within a timeless second, there is a choice to enter the world, a YES to life, and at that moment the angel blows out the candle. The about-to-be born soul forgets it all until life itself awakens that knowing, especially through love, beauty, near death experiences, traumatic loss, and even crimes against humanity.

Until then we are spared, if you like, from the enormous infinitude of consciousness. No, we do not choose a life where we develop terminal illness as a child, where we are abused and carry life-long injuries, where we starve and are enslaved. These are the result of the choices of perpetrators and society's collective wilful ignorance. Our karma is how we *react* to that. Their karma is how they treat us.

Our first experience of attachment is partnered with the influences that come with being porous. And they cannot be necessarily shut off. They just pour in. Most of us survive that exquisite sensitivity. Some do not.

As children, we must evolve to manage this initial awareness. Because we simply can't live with that much sensitive chaos. It would be pure agony until we evolve in our capacity to hold space for the 'poignant enormity'[50] of Life.

Most of us build a set of defences to protect ourselves from raw awareness - we begin thickening the multiple layers on the metaphorical sponges and filter the light. And it depends on how able or privileged you are to spiritually navigate to a place where you can soften the sponge and learn how to soften with the information that pours in.

---

[50] https://www.spiritualityandpractice.com/book-reviews/excerpts/view/14540/full-catastrophe-living

A journal process 2021/22 [51]

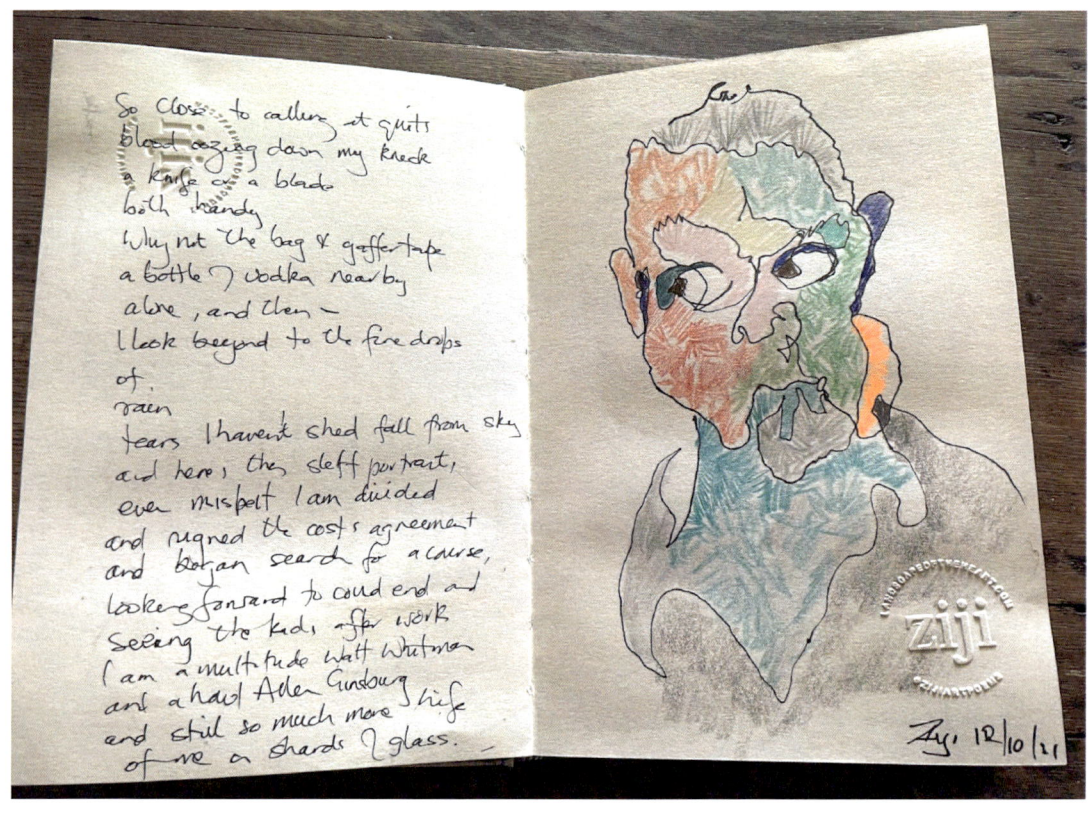

---

[51] I thought I would give you an intimate look at my journaling process. It may help you begin your own. The first image appears earlier in the book, and I drew your attention to the map of Australia. You can draw your own conclusions about what I was going through.

So close to calling it quits
blood oozing down my kneck
a knife or a blade
both handy.
Why not the bag & gaffer tape
a bottle of vodka nearby
alone, and then -
I look beyond to the fine drops
of
rain
tears I haven't shed fall from the sky
and here's this sleff portrait,
even misspelt I am divided
and signed the costs agreement
and began search for a course,
looking forward to covid end and
seeing the kids after work
I am a multitude walt whitman
and a howl alan ginsburg
and still so much more life
of me in shards of glass
Ziji 12/10/21

I don't need to do much
to disclose the lines of pain
So I say there's no scar from
left to right
but any fool can read
the mementos of the journey
on my face.
Even my feet would tell the
same story
So why do I hide the hurt
and anger in cruel lines
around my bottom lip?
The left eye is a prison
and the right a landscape
a walk in a cracked
deck of shipwrecked life.
I can still see the poet
beneath the dancing Ziji.
He lives and dies in a wink

*I don't need to do much
to disclose the lines of pain.
So I say there's no scar from
left to right
but any fool can read
the mementos of this journey
on my face.
Even my feet would tell the
same story
so why do I hide the lust
and anger in cruel lines
around my bottom lip?
The left eye is a prison
and the right a landscape
a walk in a crashed
deck of a shipwrecked life.
I can still see the peter
beneath the dancing Ziji.
He lives and dies in a wink
Ziji 13/10/21*

Now we are getting to the
trooth beneath all the charm
this guy is diabolical
almost a cartoon?
a dental assistant
or maybe anaesthetist
Thirsty bugger looking for
a
neck —
and last night meal
drippers down his shirt.
All that I could have been
but for the discipline of a good
heart, just this side of
the veil
between good & evil.

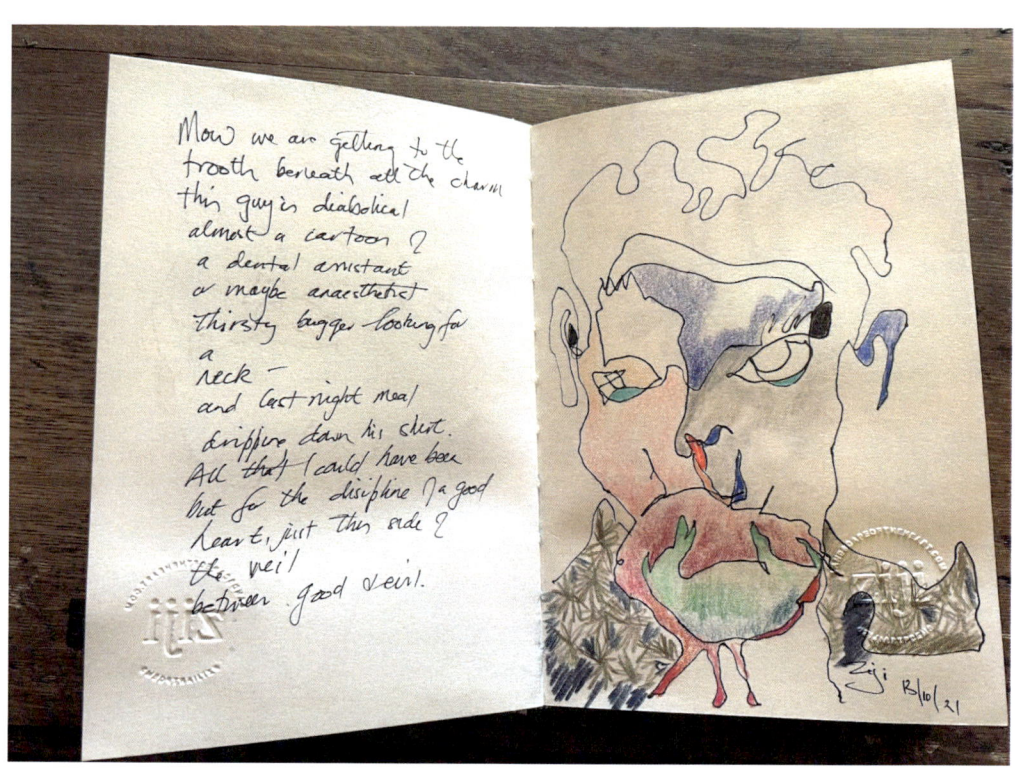

*Now we are getting to the
trooth beneath all the charm
this guy is diabolical
almost a cartoon of
a dental assistant
or maybe anaesthetist.
Thirsty bugger looking for
a
neck -
and last night meal
dripping down his shirt.
All that I could have been
but for the discipline of a good
heart, just this side of
the veil
between good & evil
Ziji 13/10/21*

Make these windows
soul to soul
soil and earth
we are bound to travel
in each other's dreams
and feet fall,
that full just right, softly
on the earth,
touching the shadow
the light
I see the sun setting
each morning we renew
I am you are us
Ziji 12/21

My darlings.
These make a life of meanings
their struggles with love's
binding
are mine and ours.
We come together accidentally.
and with the 040 years I come
to see the pattern of love
that surrounds me.
I surrender with power of
sound to erode the edges
and the tide brings waves
of gratitude and good tidings
for the years ahead
Ziji 12/21

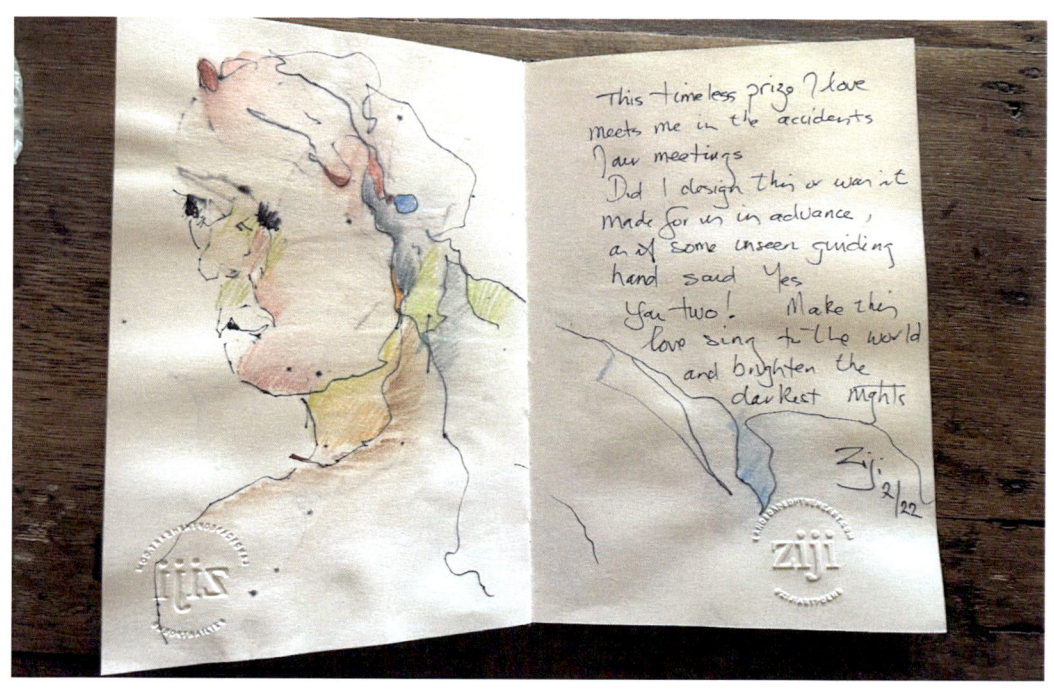

*This timeless prize of love
meets me in the accidents
of our meetings.
Did Idesign this or was it
made for us in advance,
as if some unseen guiding
hand said yes
you two! Make this
love sing to the world
and brighten the
darkest night
Ziji 2/22*

*Where one will come
gliding through the gossamer
strands of spirit
I find myself standing
with generations of men
I can be proud of
who cared for their world
and for me
unseen and un born
some burdens they passed
on for me to finish
some for me to complete
and plant the seeds in mine
timeless journey of the soul
brings me to you my love
radiant and incomplete
Ziji 12/21*

2008. #57

APPENDIX - THE ZIJI ART METHOD #58

Here are the basics for the Ziji Art method:

- Set the intention: Begin by setting an intention for your creative practice. This could be to explore a certain theme or emotion, to quiet the mind and focus on the present moment, or simply to let go of expectations and allow your creativity to flow freely.
- Prepare the materials: Choose the art materials that you want to work with. This could be anything from paints and paper to clay or fabric, musical instruments, video etc. Make sure that you have everything you need within reach so that you can fully immerse yourself in the creative process.
- Practice mindfulness: Take a few moments to centre yourself and practice mindfulness before you begin your creative work. This could involve a brief meditation, some breathing or pranayama practices like Nadi Shodhana, or simply taking a few moments to focus on your breath and bring your attention to the present moment.

- Begin the process: Allow yourself to begin without judgment or preconceived ideas of what the final product should look like. Be curious and get out of the way of the process. Let go of the need for perfection or to get to a destination.
- Let the process guide you. Allow the creative process to guide you as you work. This could involve exploring different colours, textures, or shapes, or sounds and movement or simply letting your intuition lead you. It could involve dancing, music, singing or a lump of clay.
- Reflect on the experience: Take some time to reflect on the experience of creating. Consider what emotions or thoughts came up for you during the process, and how the experience impacted you.
- Embrace imperfection: Finally, remember to embrace imperfection and view your work as a reflection of your own unique creativity and self-expression, rather than something that needs to be polished or finished piece of work.

By following this methodology, the Ziji Art method can be a powerful way to tap into your creativity, explore your inner self, and find a sense of peace and mindfulness in the present moment.

Where the intention is to access disavowed or dissociated aspects of the self.

1.	Set the intention: Begin by setting an intention to explore the disavowed aspects of your inner self. This may involve a willingness to confront your fears, doubts, and insecurities, and to bring these aspects of yourself into the light.
2.	Practice mindfulness: Take some time to practice mindfulness and become present in the moment. This can involve a brief meditation or simply taking some deep breaths to calm your mind and focus your attention.
3.	Engage in creative expression: Use creative expression as a tool for accessing your shadow self. This could involve writing, drawing, painting, or any other form of creative expression that resonates with you. Go slowly.
4.	Embrace the discomfort: Allow yourself to explore the uncomfortable or disavowed aspects of yourself without judgment or resistance. Breathe through it. Every PTSD storm will pass. Recognise that discomfort is a natural part of the process of exploring the shadow self, and that it can ultimately lead to greater self-awareness and personal growth.

5.   Reflect on your creations: Take some time to reflect on your creative expressions and explore any themes or patterns that emerge. This can be a way to gain deeper insight into your disavowed aspects and to better understand how they manifest in your life.

6.   Seek support: Recognise that exploring the shadow self can be a challenging and sometimes overwhelming process. Seek support from a therapist, counsellor, or trusted friend to help you process any difficult emotions that arise. In the Ziji Art method, there is often a relationship between the drawing and the poem written beside it on the same page at the same time. This is because the drawing and the poem are both created in the same moment, and both are intended to be expressions of the same inner self, reflecting the information stored on left and right sides of the brain.

The drawing and the poem can be seen as two different forms of expression that work together to create a unified whole. Left and right brain taking turns, sometimes in synch. The drawing may be an expression of the artist's emotions or thoughts, while the poem may be a way to articulate those emotions or thoughts in words. Together, the drawing and the poem can provide a more complete picture of the artist's inner self and their creative expression.
In some cases, the drawing and the poem may be directly related, with the poem serving as a reflection on the drawing or to further explore the emotions or ideas expressed in the drawing. In other cases, the relationship may be more indirect, with the drawing and the poem expressing different aspects of the artist's inner self.

Overall, the relationship between the drawing and the poem is often an organic one, with the two forms of expression working together to create a complete and authentic representation of the artist's inner self.

When the unconscious material that you are trying to access was of violation and abuse, the process of accessing the shadow self may require a more nuanced approach. Here are a few suggestions:

Cultivate a non-judgmental attitude toward yourself: It's important to approach the exploration of abuse without self- judgment. The goal is not to suppress or condemn these aspects of the self, but rather to understand them more fully. The perpetrator/s are to be judged in your own way. These are often complex situations where the simple fact is that you did not nor could ever have consented. Grooming is a particularly insidious process - a mind fuck to cheat you out of your choice, bypass your consent, steal your innocence whilst transferring the blame to you.

- Use creative expression: Creative expression can be a powerful tool for exploring these experiences. Consider using movement, music, drawing, painting, or other forms to express these aspects of the self. Prose or poetry can be an effective way to explore these themes. Same with music and dance. Consider some clay or other materials.
- Create a safe time and place: It's important to create a safe and private space where you feel comfortable expressing your experiences. This can involve finding a private location, using headphones or earplugs to block out external distractions, or even using a pseudonym to maintain anonymity.
- Seek support: If exploring it feels overwhelming or uncomfortable, it's important to seek support from a trusted therapist, counsellor, or friend. They can provide guidance and support as you navigate these complex and often sensitive issues. Go slow!
- Focus on self-exploration: Ultimately, the goal of exploring these experiences is to gain a deeper understanding of yourself and your process of healing. Focus on self-exploration and self-discovery, rather than external validation or approval.
- After-care – consider using trauma release exercises (TRE) or Havening techniques to allow the body to recover; arrange a massage in advance; a phone hook up with a sexual trauma service or your counsellor or best friend.

By approaching the exploration with an open and non-judgmental attitude, using creative expression, in a safe space, seeking support when needed, and focusing on self-exploration, the artist can access the shadow self in a way that is meaningful and productive. It is a developmental process that takes time and oodles of self-compassion.

Working with a nude model

Working with a nude model involves ethical considerations, the need for both clear communication and boundaries.

When working with a nude model, there are some poses that can elicit disavowed or dissociated parts of ones being or of the experience of shame. Here are a few suggestions:

- Twisted or contorted poses: Twisted or contorted poses can evoke a sense of discomfort or unease, which can sometimes lead to experiencing hidden parts of the self.
- Vulnerable poses: Poses that emphasise vulnerability, such as lying on the back with arms and legs engaged in different positions, can also bring up feelings of discomfort and vulnerability. These can sometimes lead to the emergence of disowned aspects of the self. Even looking can be disavowed. Being seen can arouse shame.
- Sensual poses: Sensual poses that emphasise curves, lines, and the play of light and shadow can evoke a sense of eroticism and sexuality, which can sometimes lead to discomfort in the artist. These may be allowed into awareness through gentle, calm abiding in the feeling. Taking a few slow breaths may allow the feeling to expand and inform of its origins.

Ultimately, the specific poses that elicit core issues will vary depending on the individual artist/poet, their unique experiences and history, and the model's. The key is to approach the process with an open and non-judgmental attitude, and to use the poses as a doorway to the shadow self in a safe and respectful manner.

Working with a nude model can potentially help you to access your shadow self. The naked body can be a powerful symbol for the psyche, representing vulnerability, authenticity, and raw emotion.

When working with a nude model, you have an opportunity to tap into the symbolic power of the body, and to explore your relationship with your own body, and to nudity; the erotic; sexuality, and intimacy.

The model themselves will have a set of unique skills and understandings to hold the space for you. Be curious about that too. The energy in-between can facilitate the work. Some art models also provide body work, yoga, movement or dance in their working lives.

However, it's important to note that the process of accessing the shadow self is a deeply personal and individual experience. While working with a nude model can be a useful tool for some artists/poets, it may not be the right approach for you. Some artists/poets may feel more comfortable exploring their shadow self through other means, such as creative writing, sculpture, drawing, dance, music, movement, or meditation.

It's also important to approach the process of working with a nude model with sensitivity and respect. Beginnings and endings of sessions are particularly sensitive moments. In couple therapy we often say the first 4 minutes of coming together sets the nervous system up for the rest of the evening The same goes for goodbyes.

Models who participate in the sex industry without coercion or violation

Engaging people in the sex industry as nude models has been a practice in the art world. Egon Schiele in the early 20th Century, for example, employed prostitutes clothed and naked. However, for the purpose of accessing the shadow self it is not necessarily a more fruitful approach than using any other model.

The process of accessing the shadow self is deeply personal and individual, and it requires a safe and respectful environment in which to explore one's inner self. People engaged in the sex industry sometimes have a wealth of experience in safety, consent and respectfully eliciting the expression of desires, fantasies, and body practices in their clients. This is a collaborative process.

Egon Schiele[52]

---

[52] https://en.wikipedia.org/wiki/Egon_Schiele

Egon Schiele's figurative works often focused on the human form and used nudes as his subjects. His style was characterised by a distinctive use of line, which conveyed a sense of tension and expressive emotion in his drawings and paintings. His work has been praised for its rawness and honesty in depicting the human body, often including an emphasis on its imperfections and flaws.

The Ziji Art Method, on the other hand, is a contemporary art process that emphasises spontaneity and accessing the unconscious. It involves the creation of drawings or paintings in response to poetry or prose, with an emphasis on allowing the creative process to unfold without preconceptions or self-censorship.

The Ziji Art Method is an approach to art-making that emphasises free expression and the exploration of the self. Schiele's work was created in a different time and cultural context and reflects his own artistic vision and sensibility.

Freud and Jung

Both Sigmund Freud and Carl Jung considered art as a means of accessing the unconscious, and they believed that artistic expression could be therapeutic and contribute to personal growth and development. However, their views on the relationship between art, sex, and the unconscious differed.

Freud was a contemporary of Egon Schiele, and his theories on psychoanalysis and the unconscious were influential during Schiele's short life. While Freud did not specifically discuss Schiele's work, he wrote extensively about the relationship between sexuality and the unconscious, and he believed that sexual impulses and desires played a fundamental role in shaping the human psyche. He also believed that artistic expression could provide a healthy outlet for repressed sexual impulses and help to promote psychological healing.

Jung, also a contemporary of Schiele, had a more nuanced view of the relationship between art, sex, and the unconscious. He believed that the unconscious contained both positive and negative elements, including the shadow self and the anima/animus, which could be accessed through artistic expression. Jung also believed that creative work could provide a way to integrate these unconscious aspects into one's conscious identity, leading to personal growth and development.

Jung described the shadow self as a blind spot of the psyche. It is projected like a movie onto a cinema screen, where we see it in the social world and within our distortions of thinking. The shadow may appear in visions, dreams and in those moments, we describe as an epiphany.

'He saw quite clearly that failure to recognize, acknowledge and deal with shadow elements is often the root of problems between individuals and within groups and organizations; it is also what fuels prejudice between minority groups or countries and can spark off anything between an interpersonal row and a major war.' [53]

End Notes

1 My anima, and on page 2, my introspective animus with guardians. In Jung's archetypes there is a lovely word for this duality – syzygy. It describes a yoked pair of parts within the Self, a yin and a yang. Read more at https://en.wikipedia.org/wiki/Anima_and_animus
2 http://ziji.life
3 Saskia of medicinalintimacy.com has been the model for some of the images here. Recognizable wearing glasses.
4 One of many love songs to Mary through the model. We sleep apart a couple of nights a month when she does a night shift. I find easily reaching out to her in those poems, as if I can draw her close and sleep beside her when she is away. I think it is a self-soothing process I learnt as I child without a mother who held me through the night terrors. 'I feel you climbing beside' is shorthand for climbing in bed to lie beside me. I love the big open space on her left feminine side. These spaces result from taking the pen for a walk, looking at the model and not the paper, and not knowing where it will end. See https://en.wikipedia.org/wiki/Blind_contour_drawing for more info on that.

[53] https://www.thesap.org.uk/articles-on-jungian-psychology-2/about-analysis-and-therapy/the-shadow/

5 Katherine Toka of https://followyourart.net.au/ met this gorgeous person while they were at the beach. She introduced herself and asked if she would be interested in modelling for us. Now a regular and she brings a lovely presence to the work.

6 I want to write an essay on the Muse but no room for it here. Adele Tutter has said most of it as editor of this book *The Muse – Psychoanalytic exploration of creative inspiration* 2016. However, the subtitle of my next book in this art/poetry series will be 'Intersubjectivity'. I believe that is the process between artist and muse. A term invented by Edmund Husserl (1859–1938) that pointed to the interchange of thoughts and feelings, conscious and unconscious, between two people facilitated by empathy. Merleau-Ponty (1908-1961) extended this observation to 'the body as the primary site of knowing the world. The flesh of the world,' as he called it. The perceiving body and the perceived world are intricately intertwined, as I believe are the artist and the muse.
https://en.wikipedia.org/wiki/Maurice_Merleau-Ponty

7 Every figurative drawing is to some extent a self-portrait. I imagine that of landscape artists as well. But here I surprised myself as the words flowed onto the page - like that's private knowledge you're putting out there. Credit to Saskia for breathing me through this moment. In a more public setting, I would have censored it, certainly not showed, nor read it to an audience. There was some shame about being exposed but that's not present now. Emphasising the contours of the eyes speaks to being seen. It's Saskia watching me watching her and we have an agreement to follow the shame wherever it leads us.

8 https://followyourart.net.au/

9 I leave areas wide open so I can fill with color to blur inside and outside the body. Not minimalist but wild emptiness. In Japanese kanso = no-frills, basic and clean. How can I show you Zen unless you first empty your cup? In this image I have let the green bleed to the left arm and shoulder. It's part landscape as if the body grew out of the ground.

10 That's a better portrait of Bridget than the one referred to in the endnote 14 below.

11 This was completely accidental. Only when I saw the hand coming out of the blue without a body and coming toward my groin, did I realise it was one of the scenes in which I was abused. I wonder if the absence of the hand's owner is how my brain has stored that experience so it's not so shocking when recalled. The poem then

came out as I felt into the image, exploring what the missing element is. In that sense the implicit is more powerful than the explicit, the unsaid louder than the spoken.

12 The poem is explicit, yet I don't remember that experience. My body has coded it that way, and the words point at it. I try to deny it and then remember the 'body doesn't lie' and it 'keeps the score'. It jumped out on the same day as the image referred to in the note above, with Saskia lying down, resting. Relaxation can be a trigger. Sleep certainly. I've explored that phenomenon in my novel Dream Life of Debris 2nd Edition 2023. The deep out breath and intake and then speak the words between 'emptiness' and 'gone' in the poem is as long as it takes to dissociate, a breath in and out and then, gone … out of body.

13 Our art group were collectively smashed by the rejection of the Uluru Statement from the Heart in the 2024 referendum. The room was filled with confusion, sadness, shock and rage. This poem and drawing just came without premeditation, as if voicing the collective bewilderment. It's one of my favourite images and poems in the book. The paper is an A3 MM Kraft Paper Pad 115 gsm and the pencils wax based, Derwent Lightfast Drawing set of 24. One of my favourite palettes.

14 I wrote this poem to our model and fellow artist Bridget. I read it without taking my eyes off her except to glance at the words. The image is unrelated to the poem and not representative of her beauty.

15 I put a lot of thought into that ear. Not so spontaneous as the figure itself. That's my posture curled up and listening intently to body, allowing left and right brain work together. It seems like my work is a function of listening and not insignificantly, I am hearing impaired. I remember one of my acupuncturists taking my pulse and turning his head to put his ear nearer the wrist he was holding. There's a photograph of me in the art group early in the book, left hand full of Derwent coloured pencils and body curled in a similar way.

16 I don't like this image. Part of me wants to chuck it but the poem I like and was a response to the drawing, both probably finished in about 15 minutes, hence very little additional colour. The model naturally fell into that pose. Is the arm across her face guarding against something? For me it's about hiding from being seen. In my head I heard Walt Whitman's Song of Myself - 'I am large. I contain multitudes.' And this evolved into the poem of the inner contradictions in harmony that define my character.

17 That's my late father-in-law Kenneth with the stick and my son aged 4 and wife Mary at Maloney's Beach, South Coast NSW.
18 My late father-in-law again but the image represents my own Dad.
19 Me and my Mary, love of my life, bound together. Conte Crayon Pastel on 140 gsm MM Black Paper Sketch Pad.
20 I can't remember the date on this one. I was making a series on my birth whilst we lived in Canberra. I had converted our double garage into a studio. I aimed to consciously express the internal image I carry of the smash and grab caesarean. Blood seems to be pouring out of the mouth, maybe of myself in shock. My mother bled to death. Today my style and the palette have changed. That image seems pre-meditated to me now, almost designed, a bit crude, literal even heavy handed.
21 A prayer as if spoken by my mother.
22 This is one of several images taken from my art diary. Sometimes these are from a day with our art group, who support all of us to get into the zone. This one is from a session with Saskia.
23 This model came to our group when she was pregnant and then after the birth, when the babe was a couple of months. There wasn't a dry eye in the room we were all so moved by the deep bonding of mother and child. And I think there was healing for those of us who didn't have the blessings of such a bond. Conte Pastel Crayons on MM Black A3 pad.
24 I have drifted from ink and wash and gravitated to ink, crayon and conte so I can get more colour detail down in less time. Nevertheless, I love this one on a sheet of A2 heavy weight cartridge pad 200 gsm.
25 I'm not sure of the date on this one, but it is part of a series about longing, loss, and mourning. I was sensing something in my body was life threatening. I read in the poems that I was mourning as if anticipating losing the love of my life, Mary. I listened and didn't hesitate to do all the diagnostic tests MRI, PET scan and trans perineal biopsy. Growing up in a medical family, and with a father complex, I had little trust in their industry, but I believed what the poems were saying. My prostate was cut out clean with a wide margin. I am in good health, relieved of what seemed like unrelated symptoms. My therapist Eve Marie, who worked with me for many years with tantric shamanic healing and sexological massage, was not surprised. Just prior to the op, we had a session in which I experienced something akin to psychic surgery – as if her energy had

entered the energetic body of the prostate and gently lifted it out and brought it into the light.

26 On the way to the Picture House in Brunswick Heads, I was eating a BLT sambo with a cup of coffee from Uncle Toms Pies. Feeling the loss of the referendum curling around in my brain, this poem began to emerge almost as soon as I sat down to draw the model. The image is one of my best describing the body as a landscape. The earthy colours of the Derwent wax-based pencils, and brown craft paper just bring it to life. I think it's part of how I see our lives emerging from the landscape. Mary and I feel the land where we live had claimed us from the start, and we now plunge into it with abandon like it is The Mother.

27 I titled it 'The Father' to point to the Jungian archetype, which in my case comprises a Father Complex. In me it has led to fear, defiance, and disbelief in authority. I find that more useful to me than a positive father complex that might have led to me to an overweening dependence on authority. I had one mostly positive father figure in my foster father, and two mostly damaging ones - the biological and the paedophile. 'Complexes interfere with the intentions of the will and disturb conscious performance … they behave like independent beings.' CG Jung. Complexes in Jungian thinking shape our emotions, desires, perceptions, behaviours, thought and all our interactions with the world. There's more on this subject on the web. Start here:

https://en.wikipedia.org/wiki/Father_complex

The father image here is of a shell of a man, the insides eaten out perhaps like a Mussel from a plate of Moules a la mariniere, one of my favourite seafood dishes. This is another kind of emptiness that sets up a fear of self-annihilation at the core of a narcissistic personality. They exhibit this hunger to devour any other that gets close to them, and then claim the credit for all the other's achievement and none of the responsibility for their own failures.

28 Another poem to my darling Mary, from my Artist's diary.

29 One day we had a couple modelling for us. They had previously come with BDSM gear to celebrate the Mardi Gras. But on this occasion, they modelled as a couple without adornment. After I showed it and read it to the group, the model came up to me innocently, and said he loved my work and recognised that I used this process as a kind of confessional. He worked in a similar way with his poetry, he said. What's particularly uncomfortable about the figure at the front is that it reprises other trauma images I have

created. A young me with the paedophile behind. I felt exposed, it touched on my feelings of shame. He of course knew none of the history and projected his own narrative onto my art/poetry. I was a little more careful about what poems I read after that, and yet was gifted insight into how my work reaches into the viewer's story. I can never predict the emotional engagement of an audience and am often surprised by it. I can describe his disclosure simply as an empathy-related response, or as an automatic embodied reaction based in our mirror neurons. More on that here https://www.ncbi.nlm.nih.gov/pmc/articles/PMC5323429/

30 Some of my poems come straight out of a dilemma a client shared that week. This one and the adjoining are beautiful and colourful images of a model, the first with a slightly downcast or shy appearance, almost cute and self-effacing. The second almost upside down, looking across the page at the other. I easily found the poem for the first image. It was from a couple I had been working with. Each longed for connection with their partner, blamed the other for their lack of vulnerability, and both believing they made no contribution to the breakdown. Unsafety prevailed.

These patterns are often shaped by unacknowledged early life trauma that in a way led to their partnering with a person who would feel familiar (of the family) and reproduce the exact attachment dilemma. A straight line from childhood to adulthood.

31 I deliberately put this image on the right side of the other referred to above, though drawn at different times and places. The models are not related but the poems collide as if the left and right of the cis gender divide.

32 This is a song for Saskia. Her stories take me all over the world, into places I hadn't believed existed except in fiction.

33 I gave myself these instructions to rest in the sea of wellness as I breathe through the memories. It set me up to release the image of the following note.

34 This was the first time I explicitly created an art poem about the criminal. Again unpremeditated, it just came out of a group art session. I wanted to censor it to stop it coming up. I breathed through a most sickening experience but now a year later, I am okay with it. My therapist Michelle W. wanted to spread the poem and the image all over the child sex abuse recovery network, it spoke to her so powerfully. If anyone wants to use it you have my permission to do so, provided you acknowledge the source.

35 I don't usually fill in the eyes with detail or expression as these two drawings do. Both created March 2019 at a weekend art gathering. I added it here as it speaks to my ambivalence about the paedophile, who trapped me in an ongoing relationship after I left Hobart.
36 Just a beautiful image and a poem of longing for repair.
37 Did I choose this? Always the question that each of us struggle with – was it in some way my fault. A child cannot consent to this crap, but both the abuser and the culture often blame the victim.
38 Leonard Cohen closely studied Martin Buber, the Austrian theologian who argued that the fundamental premise of all spirituality is not about religious dogma but everyday human experience. *Everyone comes to love as a refugee* echoes Buber's exile quote.
39 I did this one in 2008 in Canberra while working through my birth trauma with my first somatic psychotherapist, Mardhi R.
40 By now the face has somewhat repaired from the previous disembodied one. Perhaps there's a voice now. And yet here it is again, did I choose this? It's a powerful internal perpetrator that like a monkey sits on the shoulders and calls out blame, rather than name the abuser and claim the injury.
41 It's a threesome from an art weekend, with perhaps another group posing on the same floor. This one caught my eye, and what formed was a prayer. The autobiography of the image is straight out of my multiple relationships, that once I called sex addiction. Here I express it as gathering fragments of the past, trying to find myself in another's arms.
42 I love this one, the poem, the drawing, and the colours, not sure who the model is but the poem just flowed out of me like the tide of the Brunswick River. This is my pick of the best feeling of Mary in the book.
43 At last, the portrait has a balanced face. The poem came out of a moment of falling in love, and it took me straight to the feelings I had for Mary before she ever knew. The image has been evolving over the pages of this book and in my mind. It is the same model with long hair in the previous ones, onto who I have projected an image of myself. I look at that and I like me. Warm colours, two feet, eyes, and mouth. This guy is balanced, thoughtful, calm, and relaxed. People who know me would use those words to describe my persona. The only clue that all is not well inside there is the disappeared right arm in the blue that takes in shoulder and hair. But I think that's overanalysing the image.

44 My first wife Lorraine and I were in Aix en Provence in the early 70's. I think it was on my first trip back home to the UK. My Aunt had insisted we had to be married if we were to share the same bed, so we did. Re-uniting with my foster family after 8 years seemed to mark the end of my prison term with the father in Oz. Though this poem was written decades later, the reference to Aix led me back to a possible meaning – I decided to live my own life and not the one he had chosen for me. Even the insurmountable becomes possible when taken in small steps!

45 This and the next titled Safe harbor are paeans to Mary. The models were from a group session that so easily emitted safety, security, comfort – all the qualities I find in her arms. Secure base and safe harbor come from attachment theory. My experience of a secure base up to 8 years of age was good enough, from good enough foster parents, family, and community. This made a huge difference, the difference between life and death.

46 This image is getting closer to where the human form is part landscape. If you look closely there is an eye and a nose on the top edge of the figure, a hairline and one big bold green arm like branch that supports the whole figure. I can almost taste the colours and smell the rainforest.

47 I prefer the colours of the iPhone photo edit. Taken and adjusted on the desktop I am writing this on, I can't get the same effect. I think the iPhone calibrated the tone from the brown of the table on the left of the art/poem. In the studio I had a white background, and the image looks washed out.

48 The model and I both cancer survivors. I started at her feet and then ran out of room so put a quick head on the left, but didn't think about the poem, it just came out and I read it to her in the break. She is so much more beautiful than the image. She had feared no one would find her attractive after the surgery, proudly announcing she has a new lover.

49 To some extent every client has the potential to trigger my own trauma response. I have experienced quite serious decompensation where I can no longer compensate for my trauma history. Here is a take on the impact of working with client trauma.

'Trauma therapists are exposed … to tales of betrayal, violence, extreme cruelty, and manipulation of young children. Their craft requires them to immerse themselves empathically with the experiences that they witness. While non-therapists can listen and tune out or find some way to emotionally remove themselves from testimony of abuse, this is obviously counterproductive for therapists working with patients who have been victimized brutally and subsequently had their suffering ignored or minimized by those closest to them.

Most forms of therapeutic engagement with victims of childhood trauma emphasize the therapeutic relationship. Paradoxically it is empathic immersion that is both necessary and understood to be the portal through which harm can come to the therapist's inner life.' Quoted from Scientific American https://shrtm.nu/Dted

'Psychologists witness the immediate and long-term consequences of trauma for their clients, and frequently encounter their clients' experiences of trauma when listening to graphic descriptions of events such as child abuse, violence, and sexual assault. When psychologists put themselves in their clients' shoes through their use of therapeutic empathy, they 'taste' the same emotional and physiological 'pain' of their clients, via what Daniel Siegel calls the 'resonance circuits'. Siegel says that we 'read' our client's emotional state through reading our body's response to their stories and their non-verbal language; in this way, we experience some of what our clients' experience (Siegel, 2009)

Therapists may also experience vicarious trauma (VT).... Five psychological needs have been identified as particularly susceptible to the effects of both primary and secondary psychological trauma. These psychological needs are manifested in relation to both the self and others, and relate to safety, trust, esteem, intimacy, and control (Pearlman & Saakvitne, 1995).

Secondary exposure to trauma has also been associated with the burnout dimensions of emotional exhaustion, depersonalisation, and reduced levels of personal accomplishment (e.g., Craig & Sprang, 2010). Emotional exhaustion is characterised by a lack of energy and feeling that one's emotional resources are depleted. Depersonalisation relates to the interpersonal aspect of burnout and refers to the negative or detached responses to aspects of employment, while reduced personal accomplishment is characterised by negative self-evaluation.

Research on PTSD has revealed that vulnerability to developing traumatic stress reactions is complex and involves multiple individual factors. More specifically, it has been proposed by researchers (e.g., Yehuda, 1999) that lower magnitude traumatic events are more likely to lead to PTSD under conditions of increased vulnerability. Therefore, conditions of vulnerability such as specific individual factors are also likely to influence the potential impact of secondary exposure to trauma.

Empathic engagement with clients' experience of trauma is widely considered to be a significant factor in the development of STS, VT and burnout (Wilson & Thomas; 2004). Empathy has been defined as the psychological capacity to identify and understand another person's psychological state of being, however individuals who have an increased capacity for empathy tend to be more at risk for developing difficulties associated with secondary exposure to trauma (Figley, 1995).' Quotes from APS at https://shrtm.nu/nwq1

50 These guys are a delicious couple. I am sure they will recognize themselves. We were in the Scout Hall at Brunz. The poem came easily as I thought of the same resting pose with Mary, the inspiration for those words.
51 This poem was among the first that led me to consider here was something out of whack in my body. Suddenly I'm anticipating death? Where did that come from? And such delicious experiences I wanted to relive. Anticipatory grief?
52 And was this my epitaph, a love poem to myself?
53 The light inside the body of this one is bursting out as if I am responding to the chakras from which the aura emanates. I love Leonard Cohen's line in Anthem 'there's a crack in everything, that's how the light gets in'. My experience is of light within and out, the body porous, some body light more visible than others. I remember sitting in line at Sai Baba's ashram and seeing him coming through the entrance way. His body was shimmering almost as if spirit was coming into and out of the body. Yes, there's lots of allegations about that man, but I saw a transpersonal body emanating light. Both particle and wave. Not a devotee and I didn't believe what I saw.
54 I remembered a client of mine in Canberra, struggling with her teenage child's rebellion, which seemed healthy to me. She told me of this experience as a nursing mother, which came back to haunt her in this crisis with her daughter. She wondered how a baby could

reject her breast milk when the older siblings had not. It's called breast refusal. I don't remember the conclusion she came to, but it was a cousin of a related parental issue, where a parent loves their child but does not like them. The poem came out of that session 20 years before.

55 This place is where my love and I live. We had a massive rain event that shook the house as boulders as big as trucks, rolled down the hill at the side of the house. The atmospheric river created landslides all around our house. Took half of the orchard, the dam, and hundreds of thousands of cubic metres just below the house. We are now 8 metres from a 10-metre cliff, where the evidence of many ancient landslides has been exposed. Our place like many others in the valley, was built on land slips. The hills around us have been moving downhill for thousands of years. We knew none of this until we got up in the morning to see what all the noise had been about. Too scared to sleep in the house for a couple of months, we just held on to each other, tight. The right eye in the image is completely open to the outside of the body, a blue entering or leaving. The body porous.

56 My prayer that is an answer to the anxiety we felt for months after the landslides. Almost ancestral voices speaking to us and saying, 'no-one died'. Well one old lady was carried away in the mud, and many people in town lost everything.

57 This was premeditated drawing from a photograph in 2008.

58 OpenAI's GPT-3.0 Chatbot originally came up with some of this in 2022. I had a long conversation with it and then edited and added to it, and then out of interest, went back to ask the same question in 2023 'describe the 'ziji art method'. By GPT-3.5 they had put in guard rails to limit hallucination. Version 4 didn't even know the subject and couldn't help. Ironically perhaps, this appendix is the result of a machine hallucination with the help of a human editor. Out of respect for the machine, and with a nod to Steve Jobs, I have used a different font than the rest of the book. It is Helvetica Neue Light. The origins of which can be found on the web but here's a snippet. 'In 1959, Mike Parker was appointed director of the Mergenthaler Linotype Company, an American firm that sold Linotype typewriters, <u>the first machines to automatically assemble rows of characters</u>

Towards the end of the 1960s, Helvetica was chosen by the designers Massimo Vignelli and Bob Noorda to create the new signage for the New York Metro and the Graphic Standards Manual, one of the most famous visual identity manuals in the history of graphic design. 1983 saw the release of Neue Helvetica, an updated version of the font created by Linotype's graphic design studio, with extra spacing between the numbers and heavier punctuation marks to improve legibility.

The following year, Steve Jobs decided to include it in the fonts available on the first Macintosh, paving the way for the spread of the digital version of the typeface.'

Quoted from: https://www.pixartprinting.co.uk/blog/history-font-helvetica/

*Do I know thee
as finger touches
soul, heart
reaches for head?
Twinned loves
and lovers whole.
Ziji*

www.ingramcontent.com/pod-product-compliance
Lightning Source LLC
Chambersburg PA
CBRC091722070526
44585CB00008B/150